ATATÜRK'S CHILDREN

Atatürk's Children

TURKEY AND THE KURDS

Jonathan Rugman

Roger Hutchings

Foreword by John Simpson

CASSELL

Cassell
Wellington House
125 Strand
London WC2R 0BB

215 Park Avenue South
New York
NY 10003

First published 1996

British Library Cataloguing-in-Publication Data
A catalogue record for this book is available from the British Library.
ISBN 0 304 33383 2 (hardback)
       0 304 33384 0 (paperback)

Library of Congress Cataloging-in-Publication Data
Rugman, Jonathan.
    Atatürk's children : Turkey and the Kurds / Jonathan Rugman, Roger
Hutchings.
       p. cm.
    Includes bibliographical references (p.   ) and index.
    ISBN 0-304-33383-2. — ISBN 0-304-33384-0 (pbk.)
    1. Kurds—Civil rights—Turkey. 2. Turkey—Ethnic relations.
3. Turkey—Politics and government—1980– 4. Kurdistan Workers' Party.
I. Hutchings, Roger. II. Title.
DR435.K87R84 1996
323.1'19159—dc20   95–31967
                                                                  CIP

Typeset and designed by Ronald Clark
Printed and bound in Great Britain by Cambridge University Press

Contents

Jonathan Rugman graduated from Cambridge with a First in English and then joined the BBC as a trainee in radio and television news and current affairs. After stints on several BBC programmes including *Panorama* and *Newsnight*, he was appointed the BBC World Service's Ankara correspondent in 1991. In 1993 he moved to Istanbul as a correspondent for the *Guardian* and *Observer*. He has reported from the Caucasus, Central Asia and Middle East and is a frequent visitor to the Kurdish area of southeast Turkey.

Roger Hutchings has been working as a freelance photojournalist since 1982, specializing in reportage and contributing to many international publications. He has spent three years photographing the conflict in former Yugoslavia and has made frequent visits to Turkish Kurdistan. His work has attracted wide recognition and he has won many awards including: Nikon Photo Essay 1991; Nikon News Photographer of the Year 1992; World Press, People in the News, first prize 1994; Amnesty International Photojournalism Prize 1994; Canon Photo Essay Award, runner up, 1995.

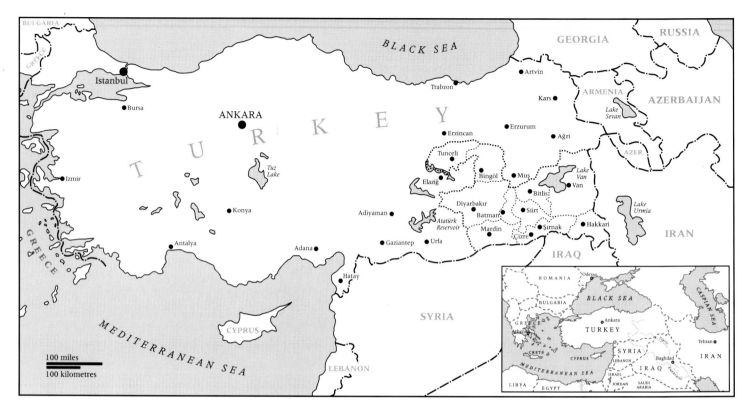

Map of Turkey showing mainly Kurdish provinces governed under emergency rule.

For Ramazan; he knows who he is.

Acknowledgements

Andrew Mango and David McDowall offered encouragement and advice, with the latter's work on the Kurds (see Bibliography) proving invaluable for my first chapter. Ferhat Boratav, Ragıp Duran, Andrew Finkel and Ismet Imset passed useful comment on the manuscript. Declan Kelly at the BBC World Service news information department and Jonathan Sugden of Amnesty International helped me with my research.

Where my own records have not been sufficient, I have relied on the published reports of several journalist colleagues, especially Aliza Marcus of Reuters and Hugh Pope of the *Independent*. Many of the 'Voices from the Crossfire' reproduced here began life in a BBC Radio *File on Four* documentary, broadcast in 1994.

I would especially like to thank Demet Kafesçioğlu for her painstaking translations from Turkish. Simon Tisdall at the *Guardian* and Ann Treneman at the *Observer* encouraged my exploits in the Wild East and gave me time off to write this book.

Jonathan Rugman

Foreword

The problems of a former empire are many. If Britain and France have encountered difficulties in finding their new place in the world, then Turkey, where the political structure is more precarious and the economy weaker, deserves our sympathy even more. Ever since its European ambitions were rejected with some brutality, Turkey has been obliged to think of itself as an Asian power instead. It has had to search for its Isamic, Central Asian and Middle Eastern identity once more, while keeping faith with the secular vision of Kemal Atatürk: no easy task.

Like most other powers that have laid down the imperial burden, Turkey has had great difficulty with the fundamental question any nation has to answer: who are we? In terms of ethnicity and culture Turkey is varied, complex and inter-mixed. Yet the myth which Atatürk bequeathed to his fellow-countrymen insists that there is a single ethnic group, the Turks. Nowadays the effects of this myth can be brutal; it can never, in the long run, be successful. While Turkey gives no legal rccognition to its large Kurdish minority, the problem that dissident Kurds pose for the Turkish state cannot be solved.

Just about every country which has tried to subsume separate ethnic identities into a single dominant nationality has failed in the long run. The Russians tried to pretend that Belorussia and the Ukraine were mere localities; the English hoped to eradicate the Welsh and Irish languages, and the Austrians Czech, Slovak and Serbian, by punishing those who spoke them; the Chinese have tried to wipe out Tibet as an identifiable entity by forcing Tibetans to intermarry with ethnic Chinese. None has succeeded and Turkey's long efforts this century to destroy Kurdish sentiment by denying that there are any such people as Kurds cannot suc-ceed either.

This book by Jonathan Rugman and Roger Hutchings is not uncritical. No one who knows the PKK as they do could possibly be starry-eyed about the violent response to Turkish persecution. Nor is it possible to avoid becoming exasperated by the self-defeating machinations of the more legitimate Kurdish groups, as they make their deals and alliances and then promptly break them. Merely because they are persecuted and denied their proper rights does not mean that the Kurdish polit-ical leaders must necessarily be saints.

The short-termism of Kurdish politics is in the sharpest contrast to the majestic sweep of their history. Anyone who has driven through the mountain valleys of Kurdish northern Iraq in the springtime knows how magnificently the wild wheat, oats and barley spring up across the meadows: precursers of the domesticated varieties which the entire world eats today. There are towns and cities in Kurdistan which are as old as Jericho and Jerusalem, perhaps older; and there are tumuli that represent settlements which are older still. The history of the Kurds stretches back to this period; they, it seems, built the cities and first grew the crops. The Kurds have a separate language and culture, separate costume, a separate consciousness. The vagaries of imperialism have carved lines across their territory and divided them between Turkey, Iraq, Syria and Iran. In the great conferences which followed the First World War it was only ill chance which prevented their joining the other ethnic groupings that were awarded national independence. Now the national urges and anxieties of the four countries where they mainly find themselves bar them from nationhood; but not, it seems reasonable to assume, forever.

Jonathan Rugman is a friend and former colleague of mine. He and Roger Hutchings, who has taken these haunting pictures of one of the most beautiful regions on earth, have together produced the best definition for an English-speaking readership of what it is to be a Kurd.

John Simpson
BBC Television Centre
London
December 1995

Introduction
A landscape of burnt villages

Smoke was rising from the village of Çelebi as we walked towards it. A thin layer of snow was hardening on the surrounding fields, and the sky was bleeding red from a winter sunset. As we drew nearer we could see that all the houses had been destroyed by fire. They were still smouldering. One man, sifting with a spade through the ashes of his smoking home, said everyone else had fled. 'The Turks beat us and kicked us, then they burned the houses down,' the man said in Kurdish before returning, almost robotically, to his digging.

Once they could see that we had not been followed by Turkish soldiers or police, several other Kurds who witnessed the destruction of Çelebi trudged over the hills from a neighbouring village to join us. 'We'll tell you what happened but don't use our names,' said one. 'If the Turks know our names, they will take us to prison or kill us here.'

Around three hundred Turkish soldiers dressed in green woollen balaclava face-masks had arrived in Çelebi, five days before the photographer Roger Hutchings and I got there in February 1994. The soldiers were angry because the residents had refused to become village guards – local Kurds paid to combat rebels of the Kurdistan Workers' Party or PKK, which is fighting for a Kurdish state in southeast Turkey.

After burning down Çelebi's houses, the soldiers set the village's tobacco ware-house alight. The mud and straw building poured with smoke until it was reduced to a giant open-air ashtray, scorching the earth black. Then the soldiers killed all the poultry and cooked up a barbecue, before leaving the Kurds searching in the dark for the charred remnants of their livelihood.

Kurds in Çelebi told us that they supported what they called the 'outside people' or PKK. Sixteen people had joined the rebels since 1988, another eight were in prison on charges of helping them. The villagers were staying with friends nearby, but said they would soon take their families and surviving possessions to Diyarbakır, the biggest town in southeast Turkey. 'The choice is simple,' said one man. 'Either we fight for the government or we leave. Otherwise the Turks will burn our houses down again.'

A child clings to a wall in Çelebi, a village burned down by Turkish soldiers.

We paid several clandestine visits to the muddy shanty towns and construction sites which form an ugly ring around Diyarbakır, where tens of thousands of refugees from the fighting have been forced to set up home. While women baked bread in makeshift, scrap-metal ovens and their barefoot children played nearby, men crowded round with stories of how Turkish soldiers razed their villages.

'We were accused of giving food to the outside people, but we never saw them,' said Naim Abdullah, a walnut farmer from Alacıköy near the town of Kulp. In October 1993, Turkish soldiers took away eleven male villagers from Alacıköy by helicopter. Their friends and relatives in Diyarbakır told us the detained men had not been seen since.

'They beat everybody, they blindfolded us and when we opened our eyes we could see our houses burning,' said another farmer, who fled from his village in

November 1993. The majority of the refugee villagers we met said they were terri-fied of Turkish soldiers and the PKK in equal measure. 'We just want the terrorists and the security forces to leave us alone,' said one man, 'we just want to lead a decent life.'

We set off on a clandestine journey across the southeast, travelling early in the morning, using backroads in an attempt to avoid police and army roadblocks. We came to Babahakı, a Kurdish village which at first glance seemed a model of tran-quillity. Women sat talking together outside doorways, as they picked cotton from harvested buds. Racks of tobacco leaves lay drying in the winter sun, but several buildings on the interior were blackened by fire. Half Babahakı's population of one hundred Kurds had fled three months earlier, after the village's Turkish teacher and his wife were found murdered.

The PKK is notorious for having killed more than eighty Turkish teachers, but a local woman who knew the teachers well said that in this case the security forces were responsible. Numan Konakçı had been teaching in Babahakı for five years and was immensely popular: he had even learned the Kurdish language. A week before the Konakçıs were shot by masked gunmen, Turkish soldiers came to the village and questioned the couple. They were told to spend more time at home and not to mix so much with 'Armenians' – a term of abuse for Kurds.

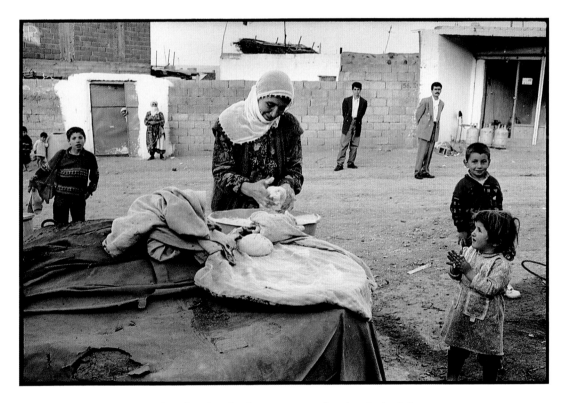

Making bread in the shanty town on the edge of Diyarbakır.

When soldiers arrived a week later to find the teachers dead, they beat the village headman and clubbed his son-in-law to death. 'Shall we kill everybody or burn the village?' a Turkish commander was heard asking on his military radio. Several buildings were set alight. One man taken away for questioning was allegedly stripped naked and tortured. Babahakı schoolhouse was now padlocked shut. Kurds who had stayed on were adamant that, whoever had killed the teachers, their deaths had given Turkish government forces a pretext to attack the village. 'We never helped the PKK,' insisted a teenage boy, 'we never even saw them here.'

In june 1995, Turkey's Interior Minister Nahit Menteşe announced that 2,200 villages and hamlets had been fully or partially destroyed since the PKK launched its war of independence in 1984. At the end of 1994, the Human Rights Minister Azimet Köylüoğlu called the latest wave of burnings and displacements 'state terrorism', and said that two million people had been left homeless by the conflict; he later came under official pressure to retract his remarks, and blamed the PKK instead.

Most Kurdish settlements have been depopulated since 1990, when the PKK increased the number of its attacks across the southeast and the death toll from the conflict began to spiral out of control. According to Turkish Government figures, more than nineteen thousand people have been killed since 1984. Atrocities are committed by both sides. In May 1993, the PKK forced more than thirty off-duty Turkish soldiers off a bus and shot them dead. In January 1994, the rebels attacked the Kurdish village of Ormancık and killed twenty 'collaborators', burning buildings and slaughtering livestock; sixteen of the dead were women and children.

Shortly afterwards we watched tractors stumbling down a dirt track leading from Ormancık village, pulling behind them trailers piled high with family possessions. But even those fleeing this PKK attack found it hard to determine which was the lesser evil – pressure from the security forces or the PKK. 'We are trapped,' said a Kurd grieving over the death of both parents. 'You have to become a village guard because the Turks force you.'

The PKK has killed hundreds of Kurdish civilians, murdering and terrorizing its own people. The rebels are as much feared as admired, and cannot be said to speak for the Kurdish majority. But evidence we collected during several difficult and harrowing journeys across the region suggested that security forces have met terror with even more terror; little distinction has been made between civilians and guerrillas. Kurds have been turfed from their homes and their traditional way of life has been destroyed.

In the town of Lice, north of Diyarbakır, it was hard to find anyone brave enough to talk. In October 1993, Turkish security forces rampaged through Lice,

Above The burned-out tobacco store in Babahakı where two teachers were killed.

Below Lice – where people were too scared to talk.

destroying buildings and killing civilians in revenge for a PKK attack. A motto nailed to the wall of Lice police station was meant to read 'Policemen are as just as judges and as loving as mothers', but several gold-coloured letters had fallen from their brackets, rendering the sentence incomplete. 'Speak Turkish to the people, not Kurdish, do you understand?' insisted a police officer during our brief detention there. The minaret of a mosque across the road was peppered with bullet-holes, and the surrounding mountains echoed with the sound of gunfire.

One building on the town square was reduced to ashes, but only one man in the crowded tea-house opposite was prepared to comment. 'The government says the PKK did it,' he said, 'but it isn't true. The soldiers burnt it down after a Turkish soldier was killed.' Spies were listening in everywhere, and plainclothes policemen bristling with walkie-talkies followed us out of town.

In the provinces of Diyarbakır, Batman and Mardin, hundreds of street killings of Kurdish activists have taken place when there were hardly any just a few years before. Many of the victims were shot in broad daylight, in areas full of soldiers and police. Turkish 'special forces' wearing dark sunglasses and jeans patrolled Diyarbakır's streets, bearded state gunmen who seemed to offer no reassurance that there was any difference between state justice and separatist terror. The moral dividing line between the two had become so blurred that Kurds were becoming radicalized and polarized, or they were caught in the middle and not sure which way to turn. 'Yes, we want to stay part of Turkey,' said Vadettin Kaplan, a Kurdish farmer who had recently abandoned his burned village for the squalor of a refugee settlement. 'But if Turkey doesn't take care of us, who will? If they treat us like this, maybe we will go and join the PKK in the mountains. What do you expect?'

Among Western governments there has been considerable sympathy for Turkey's fight with the PKK. The country's strategic importance, enhanced by the role it played in the 1991 Gulf War alliance against Iraq, means that Europe and the United States have often preferred to look the other way rather than confront Ankara on its hardline anti-terror tactics and accompanying human rights infringements.

Poised between the Balkans, the Caucasus and the dictatorships of the Middle East, Turkey presents itself as a beacon of democracy and stability in a dangerously unstable neighbourhood. It is an associate member of the Western European Union defence pact, a longstanding applicant for European Union membership and the only Muslim member of NATO. Turkey's Prime Minister Mrs Tansu Çiller calls her country 'the only secular democracy among fifty-two Muslim nations' – a unique synthesis of values and cultures at the bridge between Europe and Asia.

Unlike Teheran or Baghdad, Ankara has stood the test of time as an abiding pillar of US interests in the region. With an army of 590,000 men, Turkey occupies 'the front-line in the post-Cold War era' according to NATO's chief of staff, General John Shalikashvili. The country's political system and economy now serve as role models for the newly independent 'Turkic' republics of Central Asia, thereby countering the influence of Khomeinist Iran.

In accordance with its strategic importance, Turkey is the third largest recipient of US military aid after Israel and Egypt. On top of around $US 400 million in annual assistance, arms deals worth several billion dollars have been struck to build American-designed fighter jets and helicopters in Turkey. Germany is a major supplier of armed vehicles, while Landrovers modified to carry Turkish troops – and deployed throughout the southeast – are built in a factory outside Istanbul under licence from another NATO ally, Britain.

Ethnic and nationalist conflicts have broken out from Sarajevo in the Balkans across to Tajikistan in Central Asia, and Turkey's Kurdish rebellion should be seen as part of a general post-Cold War clamour for independence, new borders and minority rights. But as the PKK conflict has worsened, Turkey's mismanagement of its Kurdish problem is forcing its allies to consider the country as much an embarrassing liability as an economic and strategic asset.

In June 1995, the American State Department issued an unusually hard-hitting report, requested by Congress, admitting that Turkey engaged in gross abuses including torture, extrajudicial executions and forced village evacuations. In recent years Germany, Holland, Norway, Denmark and South Africa have responded to such human rights violations by imposing temporary bans on the transfer of weapons. But Turkey was the world's largest arms importer in 1994. and with America under the Clinton administration supplying around 80 per cent of those weapons, Washington has been reluctant to link the human rights abuses it documents to a retaliatory arms ban.

When US Deputy Secretary of State Strobe Talbott visited Ankara in April 1995, he advised his Turkish hosts to adopt a multi-faceted approach. 'Force alone can make a bad situation worse,' he said. 'The way to defeat outlawed groups is to deprive them of popular support by addressing legitimate needs and grievances.'

Mr Talbott was not specific, but more than half a century after the death of Mustafa Kemal 'Atatürk' ('Father of the Turks'), it is still illegal in Turkey to broadcast Kurdish, teach Kurdish, or set up an explicitly Kurdish political party. In the name of defending Atatürk's authoritarian legacy, Kurdish nationalists and dissident Turkish intellectuals have been imprisoned for crimes of thought on the Kurdish issue, and in the name of a war against terrorism thousands of Kurdish settlements have been emptied and often burned down.

This book aims to serve as an introduction to Turkey's Kurdish problem. It explains how the PKK began and relates how Turkey has attempted to deal with the Kurdish separatist insurgency. It is my view that by commiting widescale human rights abuses and refusing to contemplate cultural and political rights for the Kurds, Atatürk's children have damaged Turkey's democratic credentials, endangered their nation's security and helped fuel the rise of one of the most ruthless guerrilla movements in Europe and the Middle East. If this is so, why is the war in southeast Turkey so under-reported? Probably because the conduct of the Turkish military and government in the southeast is rarely challenged by Turkish public opinion, while the Kurdish minority has few experienced politicians and no foreign government championing its cause on the world stage. The PKK has won few friends in the West because of its violence and extremist ideology, and it is hard to imagine Kurdish independence ever successfully functioning in a region where differences are still settled by the bullet rather than the ballot box. The spectacular suffering of Kurds in Iraq, victims of a notoriously despotic regime, has earned them the international spotlight; but across the border in Turkey, perhaps there is a hopeless inevitability to this long-running conflict which keeps the world's media away.

Travelling across the southeast is not easy either, due to the military checkpoints and police patrols, and the possibility of being kidnapped by the PKK. During our research for this book we were followed, detained and turned back by security forces on countless occasions. Camera film was destroyed, our drivers were threatened, and in March 1995 Roger Hutchings and our translator were beaten up by three men. A crowd of several hundred Kurds watched, but none dared intervene.

Jonathan Rugman
Istanbul
December 1995

Chapter 1

Turkey's Kurds - who are they?

A few years ago I was sitting on board a Turkish Airlines flight from Diyarbakır to Ankara in the company of Mehdi Zana, a Kurd who had once served as Diyarbakır's mayor. As we flew above the clouds towards the Turkish capital, I asked Mr Zana if he could ever imagine a time when this would be an international flight between two separate countries – Turkey and Kurdistan.

'If the Kurdish people create their own state it will survive,' Mr Zana replied, his eyes gleaming with more than a flicker of hope. 'But it may cost the Kurdish people very much blood,' he added. 'It's up to the Turks and other peoples of the world to allow the Kurds to be happy.' At that time Mehdi Zana had spent more than ten years in Turkish jails where he was severely tortured for daring to air such views. But that wasn't about to silence him: in May 1994, he was imprisoned for four years after testifying on the situation in southeast Turkey before the human rights sub-committee of the European Parliament. 'To declare that a Kurdish people exist in Turkey, who are different from Turkish people, constitutes racist and separatist propaganda against the unity and indivisibility of the State and Nation,' read the court's indictment against Mr Zana.

In 1994 Leyla, his wife, was also put behind bars, one of six Kurdish MPs found guilty of associating with Kurdish separatist guerrillas. 'I have a husband, two children and many friends,' Mrs Zana, then 33, wrote shortly before her fifteen-year sentence began. 'I love life. But my passion for justice for my people . . . is greater. I will not bow down to Turkey's inquisition.'

There are thought to be more than twenty million Kurds spread across the borders of more than four countries, making them the world's largest nation without its own state. Mr and Mrs Zana compensate for this deficiency by dreaming behind bars of a better future; their dream is shared by millions of their countrypeople – a dream of freedom for a land which has been marked on maps as 'Kurdistan' for at least eight hundred years.

Kurdistan has always been a geographical region rather than a single administrative entity. It has never been an independent state, and it does not have borders. Today, Kurdistan amounts to a remote and mostly mountainous region of the

Middle East, straddling the frontiers of Turkey, Syria, Iraq and Iran. There are approximately five million Kurds in Iran and four million in Iraq. There are about one million Kurds in Syria and smaller communities in Lebanon and the former Soviet Union. But the biggest population of Kurds lies inside Turkey.

Turkey conducts a population census every five years, but the census questionnaire does not identify people on the basis of their mother tongue and Kurds are not recognized as an ethnic minority. So, taking into account population shifts and inter-marriage, calculating how many Kurds there are in Turkey is a tricky business. The last census in 1990 showed that there were more than 4,900,000 people living in 12 southeastern provinces which are widely accepted as being mainly Kurdish. However, at least as many Kurds are thought to live in other parts of Turkey, giving a total of over ten million Kurds in a nation of approximately sixty million people. President Turgut Özal announced that there were 12 million Kurds (one fifth of the Turkish population) in 1992.

The traditional Kurdish homeland in southeast Turkey is by no means exclusively Kurdish; Turkish, Arab and Christian communities live there, as well as more than 200,000 Turkish soldiers and police. Armenian settlements once spread across much of eastern and southeastern Turkey, but, since the deportations and mass killings of Armenians by Turks and Kurds towards the end of the nineteenth century and during the First World War, there are now hardly any Armenians left.

Kurdistan's continental climate produces wild variations in temperature, from baking summers to frozen winters. Pastoralist Kurds have traditionally moved according to the seasons with their cattle, sheep and goats, from mountain pastures to warmer valleys. Cotton, tobacco and fruit are grown in the plains. In the countryside, Kurdish society is still organized along tribal lines, with local family chiefs often assuming the role of political and Islamic leaders. The chiefs, or 'aghas', control confederate tribes and villages.

Kurds speak five major groups of dialects, including Kurmanji, Sorani and Zaza. There are so many regional sub-dialects that Kurds from different parts of Kurdistan sometimes cannot understand one another. This factor is often used by Turkish nationalists to belittle the idea that the Kurds are capable of independence.

Some Kurds claim they are the descendants of Noah, whose biblical Ark is said to have landed on Mount Ararat, where the borders of Turkey, Armenia and Iran meet. Other Kurds say the ancient Medes were their ancestors, or that the fierce race of bowmen called 'Karduchoi' by the ancient Greek historian Xenophon were, in fact, Kurds. The PKK rebellion has compelled many Kurds to think about their ethnic identity for the first time, prompting a whole host of theories: 'I'm illiterate but I'm studying Kurdish history,' a Kurdish shopkeeper in the southeastern town of Cizre told me proudly in 1991; 'We've been here far longer than the Ottomans.'

Kurds migrating to the lowlands for the winter.

Historians agree that ethnic Turkish tribes settled in Asia Minor in the eleventh century, while the shopkeeper's Kurdish ancestors were there at least a millennium earlier. 'The Kurds are like the Scots and the Turks are like the English,' the Kurdish writer Musa Anter explained to me shortly before he was assassinated in 1992. 'The English are cowardly and slippery, while the Scottish are mountain people – more honest, more courageous, more straightforward.'

Many Kurds who have migrated westwards have forgotten their language and customs, becoming fully assimilated into Turkish society. A Turk will tend to identify a Kurdish male by his guttural accent, his darker skin and his thicker eyebrows and moustache; but a Turk could easily mistake a fellow ethnic Turk from the eastern provinces of Erzurum or Sivas as a Kurd, and for a foreigner the differences are often impossible to discern.

Although Istanbul is 800 miles from Kurdistan, it is believed to be home to more than one million ethnic Kurds, making it one of the biggest Kurdish cities in the world. The population shift away from the southeast has been partly caused by years of repression and human rights abuses at the hands of the Turkish state. But the *per capita* income in Kurdistan is only about 40 per cent of the national average, and until recently most Kurds have left the inaccessible southeast for economic reasons. Many were born into the families of small landowners or landless peasants working for rich 'agha' landlords; mountain farming is a harsh and remote existence at the best of the times, so there was little inclination to stay.

The population of the mainly Kurdish province of Siirt declined from 524,000 in 1985 to 243,000 in 1990. By contrast, southeastern cities have grown in size, offering as they do stepping stones to employment in Western Turkey and a degree of safety from the PKK conflict. The mayor of Diyarbakır, Ahmet Bilgin, reckons his city has swollen from the 381,000 recorded in 1990 to over one million people in

Primitive farming south of Mardin near the Syrian border.

1995. The next census is expected to record the most dramatic decline in rural communities yet, as hundreds of thousands of Kurds escape the PKK war. It is also worth noting that the 1990 census records an average of eight people per household in southeast Turkey. The high birth rate, twice the average of Ankara or Istanbul, suggests that the number of Kurds in Turkey will continue to rise dramatically.

Rebellions

During the early days of the Ottoman Empire, Kurdish fiefdoms and emirates were granted limited recognition by successive Sultans, who wanted the Kurds' help in policing the Persian border, which had been established by treaty in 1639. The Kurds have been hostage to the geopolitical strategies of others ever since.

In the nineteenth century the Ottomans attempted to take direct control of Kurdistan out of fear that it would break away from the Empire in the way that Egypt and Istanbul's Balkan territories were threatening to do. Several Kurdish rebellions followed, as tribal and religious leaders fought to retain their principalities.

The defeat of Germany and its ally the Ottoman Empire in 1918 offered the Kurds their greatest opportunity to prove that they were not a race of quarrelsome nomadic clans, but a people capable of nationhood. Under the Treaty of Sèvres, signed with the Allies in 1920, Ottoman leaders agreed that a commission would 'prepare for local autonomy in those regions where the Kurdish element is preponderant'. The treaty went on to stipulate that if the majority of Kurds could show the League of Nations within the space of the next year that they wanted and were capable of independence, then Turkey 'agrees to execute such a recommendation, and to renounce all title and rights over these areas'.

What actually happened was very different. Turkey's dynamic new leader, Mustafa Kemal, reasserted his country's military strength, driving an occupying Greek army into the sea and setting out the country's borders much as they are now. By 1923, Turkey seemed no longer the 'sick man of Europe' but a potentially useful bulwark against Revolutionary Russia. It would not be for the last time that Western governments, and Britain chief among them, concluded that Turkey's strategic value outweighed concern for the fate of its Kurds: a new treaty was drawn up which did not mention the Kurds by name, let alone refer to an independent Kurdish state.

However, the Treaty of Lausanne, signed in July 1923, did declare that all citizens of Turkey should be equal before the law 'without distinction of birth, nationality, language, race or religion'. It is also worth noting that Mustafa Kemal, known as 'Atatürk' or 'Father of the Turks', told a meeting of Turkish journalists in the same year that 'wherever the people of a particular province are predominantly Kurds, they will administer their own affairs in an autonomous manner'.

A similar idea was being considered by Britain for Kurds living in British-administered Iraq, but in Turkey Atatürk appeared to undergo a dramatic change of heart; in 1924 he began a brutal campaign to assimilate Kurds into the new republic. Atatürk's purpose was to forge a new and indestructible Turkish nation, a monolithic Turkish identity out of the dying embers of the Ottoman Empire. For the sake of cohesion, the Kurds' very existence was denied. Kurdish publications and religious schools were closed down; Kurdish language, education, dress, folklore and names prohibited.

Perhaps just as significant was Atatürk's decision in 1924 to abolish the Islamic Caliphate, which had bound Turks and Kurds together in their shared Muslim faith. The first Kurdish-Islamic rebellion against the new and officially secular Turkish republic followed in 1925. It was brutally suppressed by hanging the ringleaders, destroying Kurdish villages and forcibly deporting Kurds to other parts of the country. Revolts during the 1930s were similarly crushed. It was not until Turkey's first multi-party general election in 1950 that dormant Kurdish nationalism showed signs of revival. Exiled landlords were given back their property in return for delivering the votes of their feudal subjects to the Government. Kurds were elected to parliament and some became ministers. But these Turkified Kurds could not form specifically Kurdish parties, and they still cannot today. Instead, everyone was obliged to embrace the official ideology and subscribe to Atatürk's famous dictum, 'Happy is the man who calls himself a Turk.'

In 1961 it bacame legal for the first time to establish a Turkish Socialist party. During the next decade, the spread of Marxism in the universities spawned a new political consciousness among educated Kurds, paving the way for the PKK. As late as 1979, a Kurd who had served as Minister for Public Works caused a public scandal – and an emergency cabinet meeting – by stating, 'In Turkey there are Kurds. I too am a Kurd.' A military court sentenced him to over two years' imprisonment with hard labour.

Chapter 2

The rise of the PKK

Abdullah Öcalan and the seeds of revolt

The PKK stands for the Kurdistan Workers' Party or, in Kurdish, the Partia Karkaran-e Kurdistan. Their story begins in the Turkish capital, Ankara, in 1974. It was there that a young Kurd named Abdullah Öcalan (pronounced Oh-jalan) invited six Kurdish students to a meeting under the auspices of a left-wing youth group called the 'Ankara Democratic Patriotic Association for Higher Education'.

Öcalan told his student contemporaries that he wanted to create a Kurdish National Liberation Movement. At least three of his friends at that meeting were to die during hunger strikes at Diyarbakır jail in 1982, but it was in Ankara, the heart of modern Turkey, that the idea of the PKK was born. That simple fact is important, because the PKK's militancy is as much a warped mirror-image of Turkish nationalist ideology as it is shaped by the experiences of many Kurds in the southeast.

Abdullah Öcalan began life in the southern province of Urfa in 1949. He and his six siblings were brought up in the Kurdish village of Ömerli, in a mixed area of Kurdish and Turkish settlements on the east bank of the River Euphrates. The region had been home to many Armenians before the massacres of 1915. 'Öcalan' means 'avenger' in Turkish. The leader claims that his family took the name after a relative was killed in the 1925 Kurdish uprising against the Turks. The young Abdullah grew up speaking Kurdish but was to forget much of the language during his teenage years. As a child, Öcalan apparently developed an interest in religion, pleasing local Islamic leaders by memorizing verses of the Koran by heart. Although Öcalan may have propagated this story to persuade pro-Islamic Kurds to join his PKK, it seems that the young Öcalan did adopt and then abandon various ideologies, *en route* to establishing his own violent political creed.

Öcalan's next inspiration was Mustafa Kemal Atatürk, revered founder of modern Turkey. In one of Öcalan's many autobiographies, the young Kurd remembers standing admiringly in front of the statue in Ankara's central square of Atatürk mounted on his horse. Öcalan claims he was desperate to join the Turkish army, the traditional guardian of Atatürk's secular, unitary state, but he was turned down by Ankara's military academy, and instead won a state scholarship to a technical

Demonstrators hold up a picture of Abdullah Öcalan at a rally in London.

high school in the Turkish capital. His first job was working in a land registry office in the southeastern capital, Diyarbakır. He came into regular contact with Kurdish villagers who complained to him about the unfair distribution of property among wealthy landlords. The issue of land ownership was later to become an important element in the PKK's revolutionary philosophy.

In 1971, Öcalan entered the prestigious Faculty of Political Sciences at Ankara University, which still prides itself on producing many of the country's intellectual elite. There the 22-year-old freshman met other young, uprooted Kurds attempting to make their way in mainstream Turkish society. Marxism was the dominant creed for Öcalan's generation of students, both Turkish and Kurdish. Their inspiration was the student events in the Paris of 1968, and it was their conviction – still held by leftists in Turkey today – that Western 'imperialist plots' were responsible for the country's lack of social and political development.

Öcalan was now in the grip of revolutionary socialism. But he remembers how meetings of the Turkish left would annoy him, with their talk of the 'Eastern Provinces' of Turkey but not about ethnic Kurds. ('He used to come on his own, sit in a corner, say weird things and go,' recalled a fellow student. 'He was a lonely man.') He dropped out of college, and was arrested for handing out left-wing leaflets following the 1971 military intervention which was prompted by extremist political violence. Öcalan emerged from a Turkish jail seven months later, describing himself as a 'professional revolutionary' with what he called a 'radical new idea' – an independent Kurdish state. 'It was my idea alone,' he later told journalists. 'At first there were no sympathizers with it, even among the Kurds. The Turks thought that Kurdistan was in the graveyard, that the Kurds had no history.'

By 1975 Öcalan's earliest followers had been imprisoned for their political activities. Having postponed his national service, he moved back to Diyarbakır, where he formed a band of around thirty Kurdish fighters. The group financed its activities by bank robberies, raids on jewellery shops and a mixture of fundraising and extortion in Kurdish areas.

On 27 November 1978, 12 members of what was now the PKK met in a village near Lice in Diyarbakır province to draw up their first political programme. They defined themselves as an alliance of workers, peasants and intellectuals, intent on creating a 'democratic and united Kurdistan', eventually to be based on Marxist-Leninist principles. The rebels listed their targets as 'secret agents, informers and security forces responsible for torture and arrest' as well as the landlords and leaders of tribes 'representing the chauvinist class'. Landlords became the PKK's earliest casualties, as the guerrillas set out to 'liberate' Kurdish villages from feudal chiefs. The first attempted political killing was recorded in 1979 – Mehmet Celal Bucak, a Kurdish MP, survived the shooting, but a blood feud between the PKK and the Bucak family began. The rebels were known as 'Apocu' (Apo-ites), after the 'Apo' nickname by which Abdullah Öcalan was known. 'Apo' means 'uncle' in Kurdish.

The rebel Turkish Kurds were undoubtedly inspired by the resumption of the long-running Iraqi Kurdish guerrilla war against the government in Baghdad. 'Kurdistan is spread over five countries and somewhere we have always been fighting,' a guerrilla leader in Diyarbakır said at the time. 'Soon it will be our turn in Turkey again, and this time we will go on to the end. We have nothing to lose.'

The Turkish army took the separatist threat from the PKK and other revolutionary groups seriously. At the end of 1978, martial law was declared in 19 out of 67 provinces, 16 of which were in southeast Turkey. On 12 September 1980, the Generals staged a third military coup in twenty years, primarily intended to put a stop to the violence between left- and right-wing radicals in which more than five thousand people had been killed over two years, but there were also fears that Islamic revivalism and Kurdish nationalism were getting out of hand.

A ban on speaking Kurdish was introduced, compounding existing bans on Kurdish radio programmes, newspapers and education. Over the next eight years more than a quarter of a million people were arrested on political grounds, primarily leftist activists and Kurds. Their gruelling experiences in prison or police custody, especially in the 'PKK University' of Diyarbakır jail, would give the PKK some of its most hardened and radicalized supporters in the 1990s.

Shortly before the military coup, Öcalan and his 'Apocu' left Turkey behind them. The PKK commander bribed the border guards at the Syrian frontier and then travelled southwards to Lebanon. There he made contact with radical Palestinian guerrilla groups and was given a base in the southern part of the Bekaa valley. Öcalan has not returned to Turkey since he left it in 1980. Yet it says something about Apo's charisma that thousands of Kurds have since died in the southeast, fighting a war under his orders.

What kind of man is he? Visitors to the PKK in Lebanon have often noticed what one called a 'touch of megalomania' in Apo's personality. Deserters from the group have claimed that their authoritarian commander brooked no opposition, and was terrified that members of his 'Politburo' would assassinate him. Öcalan has described himself as a 'man without pity'. PKK deserters say that he has organized the execution of scores of dissident colleagues. Western reporters who have met Öcalan often remark on his rambling lectures in Marxist-Leninist dialectics. The PKK's classic revolutionary dogma seems antiquated in the light of the collapse of Communism across the Soviet Union and Eastern Europe. While many Turks today find inspiration in the dynamism of their free-market economy and the resurgence of Islam, Öcalan and his followers are stuck in a 1970s political time-warp.

And yet what is most ironic about the PKK's bandit king is his very Turkishness. 'I think and plan completely in Turkish,' Öcalan has freely admitted. In recent years, he appears to have come to terms with this irony, by abandoning his goal of Kurdish independence and replacing it with a vaguely defined 'federation'. As a result, many Kurdish nationalists are confused about just what their revolution is supposed to achieve: one minute they will talk of their commitment to ending Turkey's 'colonialist oppression', and the next minute they will joke that the PKK flag is red and yellow because these are the colours of Öcalan's favourite football team – Galatasaray, in Istanbul.

The beginnings of war

In 1982 the PKK launched its first cross-border attack into Turkey, but eight guerrillas were killed and the episode was considered a failure. On 15 August 1984 the PKK tried again. The rebels killed one soldier and nine civilians in attacks on the Kurdish towns of Eruh and Shemdinli in the provinces of Siirt and Hakkari. The incursions did not come directly across the flat and exposed Syrian border, but from the mountains of northern Iraq, where President Saddam Hussein was too busy prosecuting a war against Iran to take much notice.

From the early days the PKK infiltrated groups of no more than ten rebels into Turkey. Öcalan's Maoist strategy was to create a local Kurdish army, guided by commanders he had himself trained in Lebanon. By 1991, the tactic had proved so successful that groups of several hundred militants were launching attacks on army posts along Turkey's borders with Iran and Iraq. The PKK's ultimate ambition was, and for many rebels still is, the creation of a Kurdish state comprised of Kurdish areas across the Middle East; from the Syrian Mediterranean in the west, upwards to Mount Ararat on the Turkish–Armenian border, then south to the Kirkuk oil fields in Iraq and further east to the mountains of Iran. Visitors to PKK camps have frequently encountered Syrian Kurdish guerrillas, although the majority of Öcalan's followers are undoubtedly Kurds from Turkey.

The PKK leader has directed his war against Turkey from Syria and Syrian-controlled Lebanon for more than a decade. That might seem surprising; Syria has

The Atatürk Dam, part of the South East Anatolia or GAP irrigation project.

its own Kurdish minority and signed security cooperation agreements with Turkey in 1987 and 1992. But Damascus has apparently been happy to use the PKK to destabilize its northern neighbour. Syria opposes a vast Turkish irrigation project upstream of the River Euphrates, which threatens to halve the flow of water into Syria, and Damascus has never reconciled itself to Turkey's annexation of the mainly Arab province of Hatay while Syria was under French mandate in 1939. The fledgling PKK began to repay Syria for its help as early as 1982, when Kurdish guerrillas based in the Bekaa helped fight against Israel's invasion of Lebanon. At least twelve PKK fighters reportedly died in combat.

Turkey is unfortunate in being surrounded by countries which, largely because of the colonial Ottoman past, dislike Turks and want to keep Turkey's regional power in check. As a result, the PKK has also enjoyed moral support – if not outright sanctuary – from Greece and possibly Russia. Iran has permitted the group bases and given unofficial patronage, in what seems primarily a bid to limit Turkey's economic and political influence in Central Asia and the Middle East.

In 1983, Abdullah Öcalan sent a representative to northern Iraq to sign an agreement with Ma'sud Barzani of Iraq's Kurdistan Democratic Party (KDP). This enabled the PKK to establish bases along the Turkish–Iraqi border, but by 1987 the PKK's agreement with the KDP was a dead letter. The KDP was tired of Iraqi Kurdish civilians being mistakenly hit in cross-border raids by the Turkish air force. The PKK had also come to blows with the KDP's more tribal and traditional members, who felt increasingly threatened by the PKK's territorial ambitions, its terrorist tactics and its hardline Marxism. Despite similarities between their simultaneous liberation wars against Ankara and Baghdad, relations between the PKK and Iraqi Kurdish groups have been stormy ever since.

By the end of the 1980s, the remote PKK encampment, surrounded by watchtowers in the Bekaa valley, was turning out new recruits for the separatist insurrection at the rate of three or four hundred every three months. 'Apo' Öcalan would drive to the camp in his Mercedes from his house in Damascus, accompanied by Syrian Kurdish bodyguards. Syrian intelligence men guarded the approach roads to the 'Mahsum Korkmaz Academy', so named after a PKK commander who was killed in a clash with the Turks in 1986.

Physical training for recruits began at six in the morning, followed by several hours of indoctrination in classrooms decorated with pictures of Marx, Lenin and Che Guevara. The guerrillas were told of the 'errors' of other tribal or non-violent Kurdish groups, and taught how to incite civilians to revolt. The PKK leader presented himself as a concoction of ideologies, telling his disciples that he was not only a Marxist-Leninist, breaking the mould of traditional Kurdish society, but also a Kurdish patriot and good Muslim. Visitors reported that Öcalan's fervent follow-

A state-employed village guard on patrol after a PKK attack.

ers varied in age from 9 to 50, and that they slept in tents and unheated rooms to prepare for life in the mountains of southeast Turkey. Öcalan would try to persuade his PKK to stop smoking, on the grounds that cigarettes were not only addictive but also unavailable in the snowy ravines where the PKK hid. 'One of the main reasons for so many past losses', explained Öcalan in a PKK guerrilla handbook, 'is that our people did not behave like guerrillas. I know scores of people who were killed just because they stopped at a village for a cup of tea.' Before setting off for the mountains of Turkey, the rebels would swear oaths of allegiance, promising to fight to the death for Kurdistan's liberation. Many would swear in Turkish; after decades of assimilation, it was the only language they knew.

Each year since 1984, the PKK has targeted security forces and 'accomplices' of the Turkish state, especially villages protected by civilian militias known as village guards. There were an estimated 16,000 in 1989, many of them tribesmen loyal to their landlords and wooed into state service by generous Government salaries. As the conflict has escalated, so has the number of village guards: from 24,000 in 1990 to around 55,000 in 1995. However, some village guards are known to pay taxes to the PKK, and even provide it with ammunition in order to avoid reprisals.

From November until March, the harsh winter conditions in the PKK battlegrounds have tended to reduce the level of violence. When the snow melts on the bleak highlands the war intensifies, with the Kurdish 'Newroz' or Spring New Year on 21 March traditionally heralding the resumption of hostilities.

As the number of rebels has increased, so Öcalan has found it increasingly difficult to communicate with them or train them under his own supervision. This has meant that PKK are encouraged to use their own initiative in attacks on state targets. This also enables Öcalan to deny personal involvement when PKK atrocities are committed against civilians. In 1987, the PKK began attacking schools in southeast Turkey which were considered 'tools of colonialist assimilation'. Abdullah Öcalan also issued orders that lawyers, doctors and muhtars (village headmen) as well as teachers could be considered legitimate political targets.

The rebels gained notoriety through fear. They would arrive in Kurdish villages at nightfall, at first trying persuasion or indoctrination to gain food, funding and political support. If necessary, violence was used to secure the Kurdish peasants' cooperation. Villagers – men, women and children – would be rounded up and killed. Men approaching the age of military service were sometimes kidnapped and taken off to PKK camps in the mountains. Between 1984 and 1987, the PKK's actions resulted in more than 800 deaths.

In 1987 the Turkish Government of Prime Minister Turgut Özal – who won election when the country returned to civilian rule in 1983 – introduced a state of emergency in ten southeastern provinces. An 'emergency-rule governor' in Diyarbakır was later given additional responsibility for security in another three adjacent Kurdish areas. By 1990, Turkey had the makings of a serious problem on its hands. The PKK had grown from an estimated 200 guerrillas in 1984 to around 1500, armed with mortars, light artillery and rifles. The rebels raised money through donations and extortion among Kurdish communities in Turkey and across Europe, especially Germany. Weapons were easily obtainable in the arms bazaars of the Middle East and could be bought cheaply in the Caucasus after the Soviet Union's collapse. Additions to the PKK's arsenal were made during raids against isolated Turkish army posts.

The rebels reorganized themselves, reducing civilian massacres in order to convert notoriety into public support. Abdullah Öcalan further appealed to ordinary Kurds by embracing religion more often than criticizing it. He described the 'positive effects' of the Islamic revolution in Iran which had 'channelled the feelings of the people of the Middle East against imperialism and Zionism'. More than a hundred deaths were reported in March 1990, as opposed to sixteen in the first quarter of the year before. The PKK could no longer be shrugged off as mere banditry: mass demonstrations and strikes in support of a separate Kurdish cultural identity took place in several Kurdish areas, including Nüsaybin, Cizre and Silopi, an ugly trio of impoverished truckstop towns along the Syrian and Iraqi border highway.

Cizre was a flashpoint for the PKK rebellion, as it was the ancient capital of the once prosperous Kurdish emirate of Botan. At least four people were killed there in March 1990 during exchanges of fire following pro-Kurdish demonstrations. Turkish flags were destroyed and shops closed for several days. Kurds said they wanted the right to speak their language legally, to learn Kurdish in schools and to have Kurdish names restored to their villages. 'We don't want a separate state,' explained the then mayor of Nüsaybin, Müslim Yıldırım, 'but we want the same rights as the Turks. We don't want to be treated as second-class citizens any more. This time bomb has been ticking for six years now, and all of a sudden the people of the region are waking up . . . because of bad policies, state terrorism and torture.'

One example of state terror in 1989 became well known after a Turkish newspaper dared to publish the details on its front page. The village of Yeşilyurt near Cizre was raided by commando units, who beat the men and forced them to lie face down in the snow for hours. Later they were given human excrement to eat. The Turkish Government was eventually compelled to pay the villagers compensation after they won their case at the European Commission on Human Rights. The officer responsible was at first suspended and then promoted.

By 1990, the Turkish army had deployed around 65,000 troops in the southeast. Mass arrests of suspected PKK collaborators took place and prison sentences for harbouring the rebels doubled to ten years. Police could detain suspects without charge for up to thirty days, leading to widespread accusations of torture. Human rights groups reported that 400 Kurdish settlements accused of giving the PKK food and shelter had been evacuated and destroyed. The emergency-rule governor was given sweeping powers of decree, allowing him to seize newspapers and deport individuals from the region at will. Turkish press reports could be banned if they were judged a threat to law and order. The country's biggest domestic issue has been ill-reported by the Turkish media ever since.

In the face of this clampdown, Abdullah Öcalan's revolt against Turkish authority did not die; it gained grass-roots support. Prime Minister Turgut Özal claimed in June 1989 that his grandmother was probably Kurdish, a move which seemed intended to take some of the wind out of the PKK's sails, but most Turkish officials continued to deny that a Kurdish problem existed. They claimed instead that the PKK was solely a terrorist phenomenon, sponsored from abroad.

An emergency field hospital set up when Iraqi Kurds fled into Turkey at the collapse
of the revolt against Saddam Hussein.

Chapter 3

The Kurdish genie out of the bottle

At the end of the Gulf War against Iraq in 1991, Kurdish guerrilla groups in northern Iraq and Shiites in the south took advantage of President Saddam Hussein's defeat in Kuwait to stage uprisings against Baghdad. But when both rebellions failed, the United States and its allies showed little inclination to come to the rebels' assistance. They feared that if Saddam toppled from power, Iraq would degenerate into civil war. Turkey in particular feared the possible creation of an independent Kurdish state in northern Iraq, which would inflame the secessionist ambitions of its own Kurdish minority.

Allied non-interventionist policy was, however, forced to change by television pictures of Kurds fleeing towards the relative safety of the Turkish and Iranian frontiers. At first Turkish soldiers refused to let the refugees cross the mountainous Iraqi border, but it soon became clear that there would be a humanitarian disaster if the Kurds were not brought down from the freezing mountain passes, and so Ankara changed its mind.

Operation Provide Comfort: the birth of a Kurdish state

By mid-April 1991, Turgut Özal – who had been elected Turkey's President in 1989 – and his Western allies had agreed to 'Operation Provide Comfort', whereby a 'safe-haven zone' was created for more than a million Kurds returning home to northern Iraq. By the end of July, an expeditionary force of more than 20,000 troops from eleven countries had pulled out of the safe haven, to be replaced by a coalition air force, nicknamed 'Poised Hammer', which flew regular reconnaissance sorties over Iraqi Kurdistan from its base at Incirlik in southern Turkey.

Kurds in the impoverished conflict zone of southeast Turkey looked wistfully at developments in Iraq. The Kurds there had no flag, but at least they possessed the attention and protection of the Western world. For all his atrocities against Iraqi

Kurds, Saddam Hussein had at least permitted them their cultural rights (such as Kurdish books and education) and he had discussed their proposals for autonomy. Back in Turkey, Kurds were often euphemistically known as 'eastern compatriots' or 'mountain Turks' instead.

Özal eases up

At first, international attention given to the plight of Iraqi Kurdish refugees helped trigger a marginally more relaxed attitude in Ankara towards Turkey's Kurds. In April 1991 President Özal overcame intense opposition from hawkish parliamentarians to abolish a law dating back to the end of military rule in 1983 which forbade the use of languages other than Turkish. At the same time, parliament approved a harsh new anti-terror law which provided up to five years' imprisonment for 'jeopardizing the territorial integrity of the country by disseminating separatist propaganda'. The law was later to become infamous as a means of imprisoning writers and shutting down pro-Kurdish publications. But for ordinary Kurds in the southeast, the unbanning of their mother tongue was a welcome start. 'The important thing is that Özal is breaking taboos, he has been very brave,' commented Hashim Hashimi, then mayor of Cizre: 'People are happy, there's excitement and the people support him.'

While the majority of Turkish politicians reluctantly backed President Özal in recognizing the Kurds' existence, many feared that concessions would lead to a PKK victory and outright secession. And with every passing month, the Turkish parliament grew more suspicious of the Kurdish safe haven in Iraq.

Despite protestations by Iraqi Kurdish leaders and Western governments that an independent Kurdistan was not on the agenda, the former Turkish president, General Kenan Evren, was one of many conspiracy theorists who believed there was an allied plot to resurrect the Treaty of Sèvres and build an independent Kurdish state. The memory of how Atatürk saved Turkey from dismemberment by the allies in 1919 was apparently still fresh: many Turks still expressed a paranoia and xenophobia on the Kurdish issue, more than seventy years after the republic's painful birth.

The PKK undoubtedly took advantage of the power vacuum in the Kurdish 'safe haven' to set up more training camps in the remote mountains there, and it purchased military hardware abandoned by the Iraqi army. It was against this background of Iraqi Kurdistan occupying news headlines around the world that the PKK transformed itself in the minds of many Turkish Kurds from a feared terror group to something more. It would be too strong to say that the PKK became a popular liberation movement; it had gained power through violence rather than consensus, and showed little sense of social responsibility towards civilians caught up in the conflict. What it offered Kurds was resistance to state oppression, which played a bigger part in the lives of many Kurds than President Özal's hints of reform. By 1991, the PKK no longer needed to kidnap recruits; it claimed that so many young men and women wanted to join that the training camps in Lebanon, Turkey and in the Iraqi 'safe haven' were full.

As the war intensified, it was accompanied by a rising tide of human rights abuses, arrests and deaths at the hands of the security forces, turning thousands of civilians into committed Kurdish militants. One incident more than any other in 1991 helped destroy the Kurds' faith in the Turkish state.

The death and mourning of Vedat Aydın

It was just before midnight one night in July 1991 that three men claiming to be plainclothes police came to take Vedat Aydın away. His body was found beside a road three days later. The back of Mr Aydın's head had been punctured, his legs broken and at least eight bullets pumped into his chest. The body was buried by police soon after it was found.

A month later I met Vedat's widow, Şükran, in the family village of Aydınlar, a remote and dusty place surrounded by fields of cotton and corn. 'Vedat knew the people who took him, they were from the police political desk,' she said. Vedat Aydın was 37 when he died and had worked as a teacher in a high school at Diyarbakır. He was also branch chair of the People's Labour Party, known by its acronym HEP. The HEP was a new phenomenon in Turkish politics. It was set up by a group of Kurdish MPs, disillusioned with the mainstream Social Democratic People's Party (SHP) which had expelled seven Kurdish deputies for attending a Kurdish conference in Paris in 1989.

In 1990 Aydın was jailed for ten weeks after he made a speech in Kurdish at the annual general meeting of Turkey's Human Rights Association in Ankara. But although the teacher's friends would not admit it, his sympathies might well have gone beyond campaigning for the free use of the Kurdish language to support for the PKK. The rebels were trying to build a reputation as defenders of Kurdish rights and were attracting the support of previously moderate voices: in the face of mounting Turkish brutality, moderation seemed increasingly pointless.

Vedat Aydın was the fourth human rights campaigner to have been attacked by unknown assailants in the southeast within the space of twenty days. His funeral in Diyarbakır became a focus for the frustration felt by many Kurds. More than

20,000 people attended, turning the event into the biggest pro-Kurdish demonstration anyone could remember. The coffin was draped in the Kurdish flag, and many in the funeral convoy shouted slogans in support of the PKK. When youths in the crowd began throwing stones at barricades set up by Turkish security forces, masked 'special teams' responded with gunfire, killing six people and wounding perhaps a hundred others.

As the crowd dispersed in panic, police threw teargas at a busload of Kurdish MPs who had come to pay their respects. One of the MPs was beaten so hard that he lost consciousness. 'They made us lie down in the road for almost an hour,' an eyewitness told me afterwards. 'They beat us badly. They were laughing as they shouted at us. They shouted "we killed your beloved Vedat Aydın and we are going to put you next to him".' Some of the injured were so frightened by what the police might do to them that they stopped the ambulances taking them to hospital and climbed out. Others ran down from Diyarbakır's medieval grey granite walls to the River Tigris and swam across it, spending a night in the lush fields of the fertile river valley.

Although his murderers were never brought to justice, Vedat Aydın was eventually buried peacefully, in a grave that Aydın had himself designated for the use of Kurdish martyrs. 'The state was frightened of Vedat Aydın, and that is why he was killed,' said Hatip Dicle, Diyarbakır representative of the Human Rights Association. Mr Dicle had moved into Aydın's office a fortnight earlier, after his own had been ripped apart by a bomb.

More than fifty people were taken from their homes in southeast Turkey and murdered during the summer and autumn of 1991. Some were village guards killed by the PKK, but most of the dead were Kurdish politicians, human rights campaigners and journalists. Ankara denied any security forces' involvement in the killings and refused to acknowledge that the PKK's rise was symptomatic of the hatred Kurds felt towards the authorities. The Turkish Prime Minister, Mesut Yılmaz, who earlier in 1991 had sugested that Kurdish should become Turkey's second official language, spoke of 'no compromise on Turkish national unity' and launched the first of a series of cross-border raids against suspected PKK bases in northern Iraq. 'Those murderous bandits will be punished wherever they are,' the Prime Minister said.

Turkey enters the 'safe haven'

The first Turkish incursion into the Iraqi 'safe haven' in August 1991 involved thousands of land troops proceeding as far as eleven miles into Iraqi territory. As Turkish fighter jets and helicopter gunships attacked what had been designated a

Kurdish protectorate just a few months earlier, somewhat embarrassed British and American officials washed their hands of the affair, arguing that Turkish action against the PKK was solely Ankara's business.

'I do hope the Turks have carefully exercised the legitimate right to self-defence,' a Western diplomat in Ankara told me, but during another Turkish cross-border raid in October it was clear that Iraqi Kurdish civilians were among the wounded and dead. Two American aid workers helping to reconstruct Iraqi Kurdish villages said they had been shot at by Turkish soldiers. When I visited the village of Banik inside the 'safe haven', I found the burnt-out frames of United Nations tents intended for Iraqi Kurdish refugees, and an angry tomato farmer named Ahmed Omar staring at the bomb craters left in the middle of his fields; calling cards from the Turkish airforce.

The director of the hospital in the nearby town of Zakho led me to the bed of Cemile Muhammed, a Banik survivor. Half her face and back had been disfigured, while the legs of her small son lying in the bed next to her were badly burned. 'The napalm stuck to me and I ran into the stream with my son to put the fire out,' Cemile said. Whether napalm was used or not, either the Turkish planes had missed their targets or they were trying to prevent resettlement along the sensitive border area. Allied military officers based in Zakho said the biggest PKK camps were much further west, along the Iranian frontier.

Although they were angry at the civilian deaths, the Iraqi Kurdish leadership quickly grasped the political expediency of playing down the casualties in return for humanitarian assistance from Turkey. It was obvious to Ma'sud Barzani of the KDP and Jalal Talabani of the rival Patriotic Union of Kurdistan (PUK) that without Turkey's consent the Kurdish autonomous zone in northern Iraq would collapse: Turkey was Iraqi Kurdistan's major trading partner and its supply route to the out-side world, as well as host to the allied airforce protecting the region from President Saddam Hussein.

That August the PKK celebrated the seventh anniversary of its armed struggle. According to a Turkish estimate, it now enjoyed a total strength of 1,500 to 2,000 guerrillas. Despite and perhaps because of rebel casualties, the PKK's message of radical defiance was spreading like wildfire. 'We're a Marxist party and our ulti-mate aim is Communism,' a PKK member who had spent many years in jail told me during a clandestine meeting in Diyarbakır. 'But we don't aim to transform all the poor peasants into Marxist-Leninists. There are believers in Islam among us. Many people join us just with patriotic feelings.'

Not only were increasing numbers of Kurdish civilians beginning to call the PKK 'our children', but the organization gained attention abroad. Ten German tourists were kidnapped from their campsite on the slopes of a dormant volcano in the southeast and held by the rebels for a week. Next to be seized was a team of archaeologists travelling to Mount Ararat in search of the biblical Noah's Ark. In Lebanon, Abdullah Öcalan warned that all foreign visitors to the southeast now needed 'visas' from PKK offices in Europe, staffed by Kurdish migrant workers and political refugees. But this visa regulation, like many others announced by the rebels, lapsed once it was no longer deemed good publicity.

The conservative Motherland Party Government had hoped that its tough stance against the PKK would restore faith in Prime Minister Yılmaz. But a 70 per cent inflation rate and corruption scandals swirling around the family and friends of the Motherland's founder, President Turgut Özal, were to spell doom for the Yılmaz administration in general elections that autumn.

Kurdish MPs enter parliament

While the rest of Turkey voted for parties which promised to crush the PKK, Kurds in 22 of the most troublesome areas of the southeast voted for Kurdish nationalist candidates. The Kurdish HEP party formed an electoral pact with the mainstream Social Democratic People's Party (SHP), paving the way for these radical Kurds to enter parliament.

I joined one SHP/HEP candidate, 31-year-old Leyla Zana, at an election rally in the town of Bismil near Diyarbakır. Bismil's town square was so full of Zana's supporters that barefoot children were precariously poised in the stunted branches of trees for a better view. 'I'm not afraid of the Turkish soldiers, don't be afraid of the jailers,' Mrs Zana said, addressing the delighted crowd from the roof of a pastry shop. For Bismil's Kurdish voters, Zana's credentials were impeccable; not only was she speaking Kurdish – still technically illegal in a political speech – she was also wearing a traditional linen head-dress tied around with silk strands of red, yellow and green, the colours of Kurdish nationalism.

Mrs Zana worked for *Yeni Ülke* ('New Land'), one of two pro-Kurdish newspapers which took advantage of the new cultural tolerance championed by President Özal to begin publication in 1991. Zana's background was a potent mixture of the radical and traditional. She had married her husband Mehdi when she was 14 (he was her relative and 22 years older) and both had been tortured for speaking about the Kurdish identity. Mrs Zana had only learnt Turkish during her teenage years in order to campaign for her husband's release from prison. Not surprisingly, the PKK instructed its supporters to vote for Leyla Zana and other HEP candidates. 'The PKK is working for us. Don't call them terrorists like they do in Turkey,' one man at the Bismil rally told me. When someone began addressing the crowd in Turkish he was shouted down, and the cries of 'Long live Kurdistan' grew louder. The Kurds of Bismil seemed to have become so alienated from the Turkish state that the PKK's dream of a free Kurdistan was taking hold.

Turkey's governing Motherland Party campaigned with an election promise that it would create 90,000 jobs in the southeast. It also made an election issue out of the 'South East Anatolia Project'. Known by its acronym 'GAP', this was an ambitious and impressive Government scheme to harness the Tigris and Euphrates rivers for vast energy and irrigation projects. But the plan was at least a decade away from completion and would not alter the basic fact that most Kurds were tenant farmers, working small plots of land for rich but often absentee landlords. At least five of the most troubled southeastern provinces were either too mountainous or too far away from GAP to gain any significant economic benefit from it.

The only mainstream Turkish politician who seemed to offer more than an inkling of real change for the Kurds was President Özal: 'I will definitely solve the Kurdish problem,' he said during a visit to the southeastern Hakkari province in October. 'This will be my last service to my people . . . we don't accept federation, but we have to talk of everything – including federation. This problem cannot be solved by force of arms.'

At the end of 1991, the PKK gave its followers mixed signals. General Secretary Öcalan told a rally of thousands of Kurds in Lebanon that the conflict would intensify. But in an earlier newspaper interview there were signs of a new moderation. 'Even if we wanted to, we could not break off from Turkey,' he said, suggesting the same 'federative solution' President Özal had said he would discuss. Perhaps the PKK commander realized that, with around half of Turkey's Kurds living in the west of Turkey, the other half in the southeast would probably not want outright independence, even if they actually had the chance to vote on it.

A false dawn – Süleyman Demirel

In the end, Turks voted for Süleyman Demirel, a familiar face (he had been prime minister six times since 1965) and a man of extravagant promises. Demirel's True Path Party (DYP) took 27 per cent of the vote, but lack of a clear majority forced Demirel into coalition with the Social Democrats, including the 22 Kurdish HEP MPs who had won seats across the southeast.

Prime Minister Demirel had been twice deposed by the army, and was temporarily banned from Turkish politics after the 1980 military coup, so there were great hopes that his reformist zeal was genuine when he pledged an end to police torture, and an overhaul of Turkey's authoritarian military constitution. A Kurdish-born Human Rights Minister was appointed, although he was to resign complaining that he had neither enough funding or authority to do his job properly. In Istanbul, a Kurdish cultural institute was opened, although it was not allowed to hang a sign outside its door saying what it was.

More positively, Turkey's most controversial maximum security prison was closed, following allegations that over a hundred prisoners – including PKK members – had been tortured there within the space of a month in 1991. But in the week of the prison's closure, a Turkish sociologist named Ismail Beşikçi was arrested on charges of 'spreading separatist propaganda' because of a book he had written on the Kurdish problem. Mr Beşikçi had already spent ten years in jail for his books on Kurdish history. By 1995, so many court cases had been opened against him that he was expected to spend the rest of his life behind bars.

Prime Minister Demirel was at his mouldbreaking best when he said he recognized the 'Kurdish reality'. 'We used to say there are no Kurds, everyone is Turkish,' Demirel explained. 'What we are now saying is that there are different people coming from different origins. They should speak their language and develop their folklore, and then they should be free.'

By 1995 Mr Demirel had backtracked, claiming that the threat of Kurdish separatism meant that there were 'no Kurdish rights', but even back in 1991 the Prime Minister's words did not seem to amount to much: unlike President Özal, Demirel ruled out the possibility of Kurdish-language television. I asked the new Prime Minister if he could foresee a time when flight departures from Diyarbakır would be announced in Kurdish as well as Turkish, and he said no.

Some of the newly elected Kurdish MPs were determined to ride the wave of Kurdish nationalist feeling, but it was a wave that Ankara would not tolerate for long. Leyla Zana resigned from the Social Democrats (SHP) after she caused uproar by speaking a few Kurdish words during the swearing-in ceremony in Parliament.

Vedat Aydın's friend Hatip Dicle also resigned from the SHP after telling fellow MPs that he was only reading the oath of allegiance to Atatürk and 'the indivisible integrity of the country and the nation' under constitutional duress. Mr Dicle further infuriated many Turks after he was quoted as saying that 'we have to support the armed guerrillas because we [the Kurds] are met with force and torture'.

In the southeast, thousands of troops were put on alert in anticipation of violence during the Kurdish New Year on 21 March 1992. 'The occasion will be an overwhelming uprising . . . it will be a big explosion,' warned a PKK spokesman in Lebanon. By now the rebels were so strong in the small towns of Idil, Cizre and Şırnak near the Iraqi border that Turkish security forces dared not venture out at night.

Death in Cizre

I arrived in Cizre on the eve of Newroz to find that the PKK had already begun celebrating in its own grim fashion. Thirty people had been killed in violence that week. The latest PKK victims were three village guards, found hanging from town lamp-posts. When the bodies were cut down it was discovered that their mouths were stuffed full of banknotes. There was the equivalent of £UK 120 in each mouth – a village guard's monthly salary.

The local Kurdish MP, Orhan Doğan, asked the army and police to stay relaxed and told the people that the slightest provocation could result in a massacre by the security forces. Armoured cars occupied the town square, a military helicopter hovered overhead and soldiers watched the main roads through binoculars from hill-tops and flat-roofed houses. Coachloads of military reinforcements were seen racing through the town, bound for other Kurdish troublespots, but otherwise Cizre was empty. Iron shutters had slammed down over the cafes and vehicle repair shops along the high street, and the sky was blackened by plumes of smoke rising from smouldering rubber tyres.

'There will be shootings and deaths if the people here go shouting slogans outdoors,' a shopkeeper warned me. '99 per cent of people here support the PKK, including me.'

Looming behind Cizre is Cudi mountain, a notorious PKK hideout which has been repeatedly bombed by the Turkish airforce. Cudi is riddled with caves and man-made bunkers where the PKK stores food and ammunition. But on the eve of Newroz in 1992 the rebels had come down from the mountain and were preparing for battle in Cizre itself. That night the town echoed with the sound of weapons fired into the air in celebration of the festival, while women and children sang and danced around bonfires in the back streets, ululating Kurdish warcries.

The next day a crowd of around 2,000 marched from Cizre's graveyard through the centre of town. They were screaming Kurdish slogans, hurling abuse at the security forces and waving posters of Apo Öcalan. Children joined in, wearing jumpers, scarves and socks in the national colours and giving press photographers victory salutes. 'Biji Apo!' ('Long Live Apo!'), the crowd shouted, 'Biji Kurdistan!'

When the security forces demanded that the banners be handed over, the crowd staged a sit-in protest on the street. Then gunfire was heard at the other end of town and most of the demonstrators ran for cover. Young Kurdish men dragged rusty petrol tanks into the road to stop armoured cars from advancing through smokescreens of teargas.

As dusk fell, the army withdrew from the town centre and the PKK came out from the shadows. Men with faces hidden in their scarves opened fire on a police

The streets of Cizre during Newroz 1995.

station and a tank depot on the outskirts of town. Whenever tanks or armoured cars approached Cizre's central square they were met with gunfire, and sped away again. Journalists took cover on the roof of a hotel; one Turkish press photographer who ventured on to the street a few days later was shot dead by the security forces.

At least fifty people were killed across the southeast that Newroz weekend. There were several reports that crowds of demonstrators were shot at by state forces, but it was also clear that the PKK had usurped the New Year celebrations to stage an attempted 'intifada' or 'serhildan' in Kurdish.

In the town of Nüsaybin near the Syrian border, an official investigation recorded that nine demonstrators had died when they were crushed by Turkish armoured cars. The mayor said that more had drowned after throwing themselves into the river to escape the bullets. 'It was like a traffic accident,' the regional governor explained to me later, but when I passed on that comment to Nüsaybin's mayor he could only laugh in reply.

I drove from Cizre to Nüsaybin in a convoy of journalists and human rights activists the day after Newroz. One of the traffic policemen patrolling the highway was so enraged at the violence that he formed us into a line at the roadside and began kicking us and hitting us in the face. 'Where are the human rights campaigners when policemen are getting killed?' the policeman shouted, finally holding a gun to a Turkish journalist's head before he let us go. Prime Minister Demirel and the head of Turkey's police force later apologized for the incident, but it seemed to say much about the lawlessness of the southeast that the enraged traffic policeman was still on duty in Nüsaybin when I visited the town three months later.

A group of radical Kurdish MPs responded to the New Year's violence by resigning from the junior coalition partner, the Social Democrats. Although more than 25 per cent of MPs in the Turkish parliament claimed to be Kurdish, including the Social Democratic Foreign Minister Hikmet Çetin, the departure of Kurdish nationalists from the Government killed off any hope there might have been for discussions on Kurdish grievances with elected representatives. Instead, Prime Minister Demirel expressed his continuing faith in the Turkish army and police and projected the Kurdish problem as being nothing other than terrorism manufactured abroad. 'It is shameful that our neighbours send murderers into our country,' Mr Demirel said, announcing that the Iraqi border would be made so secure 'that not even a bird can cross' and that the PKK would be hit 'in the Bekaa if need be'.

Iraqi Kurds, mindful of Turkey's importance, condemned the PKK in the strongest terms yet. 'The PKK have a self-righteous regard for themselves as the sole representatives of Kurds everywhere,' said Ma'sud Barzani, head of the Kurdistan Democratic Party of Iraq. 'We will not accept the dictatorship of Öcalan. He has not been to Kurdistan in years. He has not seen a battle in his life.'

Barzani claimed that there was strong evidence that Iraqi intelligence had been assisting the PKK since 1990, out of revenge for Turkey's compliance with United Nations sanctions against Baghdad. But after talks with Foreign Minister Çetin, Mr Barzani tempered his support for Turkey by warning against more bombing raids in Iraq. 'They missed their targets and injured our civilians,' he said. 'I have never seen in military history a successful example of uprooting a guerrilla group from the air.'

Mr Demirel was reportedly pleased with an opinion poll he commissioned in 1992 which showed that 70 per cent of people living in the southeast wanted to stay part of Turkey. The Prime Minister responded by announcing a 'golden year' for the Kurds. Unemployment benefit would be given to 700,000 young people in the area, and a thousand new jobs were promised to the town of Siirt. 'Complete safety will be established and then the security forces will be withdrawn,' Mr Demirel said. Things seemed to be going well with Syria, after a meeting between Turkey's Interior Minister and President Hafiz al-Asad. The Syrians ordered the PKK to close down its camp in Lebanon, albeit temporarily. Damascus was apparently eager to enlist Washington's support in ending Israel's occupation of the Golan Heights.

In June 1992, nearly three hundred people were reported killed in the southeast. The greatest contributor to the rising death toll appeared to be a change in PKK tactics. Since the March Newroz, the PKK had launched hit-and-run attacks on more than forty border posts, involving hundreds of men and women. The number of PKK dead caused Ünal Erkan, the former Turkish police chief and now regional governor in the southeast, to announce with confidence that the PKK would soon be extinct. 'In one attack they brought four hundred people across and lost almost half of them,' he told me. 'They've understood that they can't be successful inside the country so they prefer attacking frontier posts.'

But the PKK offensive was not the dying gasp of the organization. Perhaps it revealed Abdullah Öcalan's political myopia, or that the PKK was now strong enough to send hundreds of rebels to their deaths for the cause. Mahmut Alinak, a Kurdish MP for Şırnak near the Iraqi border, reckoned that nearly two thousand Kurds had escaped to the mountains to join the PKK in the four months since March 1992. In a bizarre reversal of the Iraqi Kurdish exodus of the year before, Mr Alinak said that a trickle of Turkish Kurdish refugees had entered the Iraqi 'safe haven' to escape the fighting. (By 1995 some 10,000 Turkish Kurds were reckoned to be living in northern Iraq.)

The unprecedented military clampdown in the southeast meant that Prime Minister Demirel's plan to win over Kurdish hearts and minds seemed bound to fail.

More than a hundred people were assassinated by unknown assailants in the first eight months of 1992. The killings were usually carried out by a single assassin in broad daylight, and many of the victims had earlier been threatened, detained or tortured by Turkish police. One such case was that of Ramazan Sat, detained by police on suspicion of harbouring members of the PKK. According to a complaint he submitted to the pubic prosecutor in the town of Batman, Sat was beaten, stripped, soaked with water and given electric shocks to his penis and toes. Sat quoted police as saying, 'The next time we will not take you from your house. We shall kill you in the street when nobody is watching.' Exactly three months later, Sat was attacked in the street and eventually died in hospital.

With Mr Demirel's 'golden year' turning out to be one of the worst, President

Özal called an emergency Cabinet meeting to discuss the violence. More than four thousand people had been killed since 1984, a quarter of them in the previous six months. The Government promised more economic investment in the southeast, but as long as the PKK burned down factories and government buildings including schools, there seemed little sense in throwing money at Kurdish grievances. 'Many problems would be solved much more easily', President Özal concluded after a visit to Kurdish areas near the Iranian border, 'if half a million people left here and moved west. It is very mountainous here, and in the end people will move west.'

The shelling of Şırnak

Kurds had been moving westwards in search of work for decades, but human rights groups feared that the security forces were trying to speed up the migration and erode the PKK's regional powerbase by forcing the population out. In August 1992, some 25,000 civilians fled from Şırnak, an Alpine smuggling town near the Iraqi border, after Turkish tanks shelled shops and houses.

The shelling was sparked off by a PKK attack, and the ensuing gun battles lasted for more than forty hours. Fourteen civilians were killed, telephones and electricity were cut and a curfew was declared. But with just four security personnel listed among the dead, the Government's claim that a massive PKK attack was responsible for the destruction seemed unlikely. Eyewitnesses, including local officials, said that Turkish soldiers had set shops alight with petrol. The town's governor, Mustafa Malay, admitted that the security forces 'did not establish targets properly' and that his 'conscience was not clear'.

Şırnak is so high up in the mountains that for much of the time it sits under a blanket of fog. The PKK was undoubtedly powerful in the town. The rebels levied their own car tax there, and when 'Apo' Öcalan was interviewed on Turkish television for the first time in 1992, admiring Kurds in Şırnak told me they had gathered around their sets to watch. 'Ask the people what life is like here!' insisted the police chief amid the crackle of men with walkie-talkies. The town was so full of police, special commandos and plainclothes security men that no resident of Şırnak was in a position to say very much.

Turkey re-invades northern Iraq

By October 1992 the patience of the army and politicians was running out. The PKK shot dead forty villagers, half of them women and children, in the remote Kurdish hamlet of Cevizali in Bitlis province. The village guard militia had put up a fight but eventually ran out of bullets. The solution, according to the armed forces chief General Doğan Güreş, was to pour in more troops to the southeast – 100,000 men backed by 34,000 village guards. Some 50,000 mines were to be laid along the Iraqi border.

There was no point in 'swatting the mosquitoes', Prime Minister Demirel said, it was time to 'drain the swamp'. And so at least 20,000 troops advanced across the Iraqi border in an attempt to flush out the rebels and obliterate them. This time the Iraqi Kurds joined the fight against the PKK, after an intimidation campaign by Öcalan's rebels had prevented lorry drivers from entering the 'safe haven' with vital winter supplies. Western diplomats in Ankara gave tacit support to the Turkish operation, hoping that, with the PKK on the run, Ankara might be sufficiently confident to implement democratic reforms. After the military incursion was over a new law was indeed passed, cutting detention periods for suspects and granting them access to lawyers during police interrogation. But human rights organizations were appalled to find that 'terrorist' crimes were specifically excluded from the new legislation, so that Kurdish suspects were still liable to be tortured.

At least a thousand PKK were reported killed in Turkey's Iraqi operation. Although the PKK disputed that figure, the number of clashes in the southeast temporarily declined. Many rebels had escaped across the snow-covered mountains to regroup over the winter. The more dead PKK there were, the more embittered Kurdish brothers and sisters there were, determined to join the organization and seek revenge.

Many Turks still refused to acknowledge that beyond PKK terror, a Kurdish political consciousness had been awakened which brute force could not put back to sleep. It was something they simply could not understand, brought up on the Atatürkist doctrine that everyone in Turkey was first and foremost a Turk. Although the jingoistic Turkish media told the general public about PKK violence and mounting casualties, human rights abuses by the security forces were under-reported or denied. As a regular visitor to the remote southeast, an area most people in Istanbul or Ankara rarely had cause to visit, I felt witness to a massive cover-up.

There were a few voices crying in the wilderness – Turkish left-wing intellectuals, many of whom had been jailed during the periods of military intervention, warned that Turkey could not stop the PKK solely by military means. A number of youthful and Western-educated politicians agreed: 'We must acknowledge the hidden and fast-rising separation [between Turks and Kurds] and accept Kurdish political rights,' advised Adnan Kahveci, a former finance minister known to be close to President Özal. 'Otherwise we will have civil war very soon.'

Ceasefire

By the end of 1992 Abdullah Öcalan's forces had suffered a serious setback. On top of the thousands reportedly killed inside Turkey and in northern Iraq, another 1,500 PKK under the command of Öcalan's younger brother Osman had surrendered to the Iraqi Kurds and agreed not to attack Turkey from Iraqi territory. In March 1993 – usually the time for a spring offensive – the PKK leader was persuaded by Jalal Talabani of the Iraqi Patriotic Union of Kurdistan to declare a ceasefire. Donning a double-breasted suit and tie instead of his usual battle fatigues, Öcalan appeared at Mr Talabani's side in front of a press conference in Lebanon and sued for peace.

Öcalan repeated that he no longer sought independence and announced that his ceasefire would stretch from 20 March – the eve of the Kurdish Newroz – until 15 April. It was to be a major test of whether the security forces and the PKK could refrain from violence, and it also forced Ankara into the spotlight: Turkey had to make the next move.

In Cizre, many people were so traumatized by the deaths of the year before that they did not celebrate the 1993 Newroz on the streets. In one incident Kurds threw stones and the police opened fire, but across the southeast only relatively minor clashes were reported: the ceasefire appeared to be having an effect. After the loss of nearly 6,000 lives since 1984, there was the hope of peace. 'People are tired and fed up,' explained Cizre's then mayor, Hashim Hashimi. 'They are relieved and pleased that [the PKK] has taken on a political character. Most people don't want a separate state. They want their basic rights.' Senior government officials hinted at steps to win over moderate Kurds and to bring extremists back from the brink of PKK membership. There was talk of lifting bans on Kurdish place-names, family names, and possibly Kurdish broadcasting. The American State Department and British Foreign Office urged Ankara to make a positive response.

But Ankara was unprepared to lose face, and wanted the PKK either to surrender or be militarily crushed. 'They must realize that 8,000 to 10,000 men hiding in the mountains armed with a few automatic weapons will get nowhere,' Prime Minister Demirel said.

The PKK was similarly suspicious of peace. Comrade Çiçek, one of many women rebels at a PKK camp in northern Iraq, said she would obey Apo but warned that 'if the Turkish government continues with treachery, our guns cannot remain silent for long'.

Abdullah Öcalan then announced that his ceasefire was indefinite – but his list of demands was a long one. He wanted a free Kurdish press, Kurdish television, the abolition of the village guard system, and compensation for displaced people which would allow them to return to their homes. It was too much to ask of Turkey, and anyway too late; the next day, on 17 April 1993, President Özal, the man who seemed best placed to negotiate a solution to the Kurdish crisis, died of a heart attack.

Özal's death was undoubtedly a blow to the resolution of the Kurdish problem; not because he had any magic wand to wave which would persuade parliament and the military of the need for reform, but because many Kurds pinned their hopes on Özal, and with his loss those hopes were dashed. In a letter to Süleyman Demirel published after Özal's death, the President had warned that the Kurdish issue went 'way beyond the simple dimensions of terrorism' and was 'perhaps the most significant problem in the republic's history'.

The hope that died

The PKK ceasefire finally ended on 24 May when the rebels massacred 33 unarmed and off-duty Turkish soldiers outside the town of Bingöl. Apo Öcalan said the attack had been in response to continued Turkish military operations against Kurdish civilians and that the ceasefire was technically still on; but of course by now it was not. Ankara dismissed the PKK truce as a ploy to train new recruits and re-supply.

In June 1993 the PKK resumed what Öcalan called 'comprehensive war' in a campaign which would be the 'fiercest of all'. 'Thousands, tens of thousands will suffer,' he told a press conference in Lebanon. 'We have mobilized more than 10,000 of our followers.' The army stepped up its counter-insurgency, and three hundred deaths were reported in the fortnight of clashes which followed the Bingöl massacre. 'Some will go to jail, some will disappear among us, and the rest – to the cemetery,' said the southeastern regional governor, Ünal Erkan.

Prime Minister Demirel was elevated to the presidency following Turgut Özal's death. The True Path Party chose the former Finance Minister Mrs Tansu Çiller as its new leader and Turkey's first woman Prime Minister. During a speech in parliament in the month of her election, Mrs Çiller aired the possibility of allowing Kurdish education and broadcasting, but she soon came under pressure from President Demirel and the military to drop the idea; Çiller was an economics professor and a fresh face in Turkish politics, a member of the Istanbul elite with insufficient authority or experience to stamp her own ideas on the resolution of Turkey's biggest domestic problem.

'Turks and Kurds are all the same,' she told a meeting during her first visit to the southeast as leader, adding (as previous prime ministers had done) that she would 'embrace the people' but 'not give in to terrorism'. Her Government approved a $US 220 million development package for Hakkari and Şırnak provinces, including asphalt roads, livestock production and carpet-weaving projects. But later that year Çiller's recovery package was suspended: money paid out for contracts and wages was being extorted by the PKK.

Öcalan's 'bloodiest summer ever'

Up to now Turks living in the west of the country had been able to detach themselves from the distant bloodshed in the mountains. But although tough military measures had contained the insurrection, they could not prevent traces of it from appearing elsewhere. Abdullah Öcalan announced in Lebanon that Turkey's tourism industry, which had earned Turkey $US 4 billion in 1992, was a legitimate target.

PKK explosions in the coastal resort of Antalya on 27 June 1993 killed one person and left 46 injured, including 21 foreigners. Another six tourists in the crowded port of Kuşadası were among the injured when a bomb went off in a rubbish bin. Tourists were also hurt when devices exploded outside major historical sites in Istanbul. Turkey's tourism industry was only beginning to recover from the crippling effects of the Gulf War. Prime Minister Çiller claimed after the bombings that the PKK was responsible for a billion dollars' worth of damage to the economy. One major hotelier in Antalya said he had lost $US 100,000 in cancelled bookings over just two weeks.

The PKK attracted further international publicity by resuming the kidnapping of tourists in the southeast. Nineteen were taken that summer, but all were released unharmed. Two 28-year-old British bicyclists, David Rowbottom and Tania Miller, endured five weeks in captivity, including forced mountain marches, bomb attacks by Turkish jets, food poisoning and the pleasures of snake and hedgehog at mealtimes. The Britons said they were forced to wear uniforms stripped from dead Turkish soldiers, and that some of the Kurds who were holding them were as young as 11.

On 1 September Mrs Çiller told her parliamentary MPs that about 1,500 people had died in the previous six weeks, including 378 civilians. In one incident, the PKK entered the village of Başbağlar in Erzincan province, herded 27 men into a mosque and shot them dead.

The office of *Özgür Gündem* in Diyarbakır. The pictures are of dead or missing
journalists who worked on *Gündem*.

Özgür Gündem: a dangerous newspaper

In August 1993, a 22-year-old Kurdish journalist named Aysel Malkaç walked out
of her office into a tree-lined street in Istanbul. A detainee at Istanbul police headquarters claimed to have seen Malkaç in custody there a few days later, but her colleagues never saw her again and assumed with good reason that she was dead.

Since the May 1992 launch of *Özgür Gündem* ('Free Agenda'), at least eight of
the newspaper's journalists and distributors had been killed in mysterious circumstances. One man, Hafiz Akdemir, was shot dead shortly after he had published an
article on the very subject of such mystery murders. Akdemir's burial took place
under police supervision: when relatives tried to pick him up from the morgue,
they say they were beaten up. Other journalists were bundled into cars or shot in
the street.

Özgür Gündem was a Turkish-language newspaper with a circulation of more than 25,000 in Turkey and among Kurdish communities in Europe. The paper was dedicated to investigating and publicizing human rights abuses committed by the security forces in the southeast. On one infamous occasion it published a picture of a dead PKK rebel tied to a rope being dragged behind an armoured car. The paper had an unrivalled network of contacts in the towns and villages where the PKK recruited. The PKK's commander, Abdullah Öcalan, even penned a column under a false name, and the paper's critics called it with some justification the 'PKK daily'.

'I try not to go out on my own or at night,' said Gülten Kışanak, one of *Gündem*'s editors in Istanbul. Four of her editorial colleagues were serving jail sentences, and the paper was frequently being confiscated or prevented from reaching its Kurdish audience in the southeast. In January 1993 the paper had voluntarily closed for four months because the pressure of killings, arrests and police harassment had become too much.

In December 1993 a Turkish anti-terror squad raided the paper's Istanbul office and detained over a hundred people for questioning. Turkish police said they confiscated handguns, medical supplies, gas masks, and documents including a dead Turkish soldier's identity card – all of which apparently proved that *Gündem* was connected to the PKK.

'Nonsense,' said Haluk Gerger, the paper's acting editor, who would soon end up in prison himself on charges of separatism. 'The PKK are central actors in the Kurdish question. We criticize them, but we don't criticize them the way the state wants us to.'

By April 1994 *Özgür Gündem* had given up its struggle for survival: seventeen of its journalists and distributors had been killed, and 336 court cases had been opened against it. The paper stood accused of 'portraying Turkish citizens as Kurds', and using the words 'Kurd' and 'Kurdistan' in ways that defied Turkey's constitutional definition of itself as a unitary state. 'If you say you are a Kurd, all doors are shut in your face,' concluded a member of the paper's staff.

Death in Batman

During 1992 and 1993, the town of Batman in southeast Turkey earned a reputation as one of the Kurdish conflict's most dangerous troublespots. More than 180 civilians, including several pro-PKK journalists and politicians, were killed by unidentified assailants in the Batman area. The most famous to die in Batman was Mehmet Sincar, an MP for the pro-Kurdish DEP or Democracy Party, which replaced the HEP after it was closed down for 'separatism' in July 1993. In September that year, Mr Sincar and one of his party officials were shot dead by

The sister of Mehmet Sincar, an MP murdered in Batman.

three gunmen one Saturday afternoon as they were walking through Batman's jostling bazaar.

Sincar was the fifty-fourth member of his party to be killed in just over two years. In fact, he had gone to Batman to attend the funeral of another assassinated DEP member. People in the town wanted to know how Mehmet Sincar could have been killed in broad daylight, and why the MP's police escort allegedly evaporated before his murder took place. Sitting on stools in the DEP Party office were three unshaven Kurds, sipping glasses of tea and wondering who would be next. 'Everybody knows who is doing it,' one man told me. 'Walk down the street. How many police can you see? Fifty. How else could the killers get away?'

Two years earlier Batman had been a town where people sought safety. It was relatively prosperous because of a mixture of state investment and private enterprise, and because of the minor oilfields surrounding the town. Kurdish villagers had flooded in with their livestock, escaping the rural battlefields of the PKK conflict. Government officials said that Batman's population has risen by 100,000 to 250,000 in just three years.

The chief of Batman police agreed to see me, providing a welcome rest for the plainclothes policemen who had been on my tail ever since I arrived. 'If people in

Batman knew police were doing the killing, they would kill us back,' the chief argued, 'but they don't.'

Sipping orange juice beneath a portrait of Atatürk, the chief explained that some of the deaths were caused by in-fighting between PKK groups, Kurdish mafia groups or in traditional Kurdish blood feuds. His other explanation (and one popular in Ankara) was that 'outside forces' were behind the killings – Armenia, Iraq, Syria and Iran, unfriendly neighbours using the PKK to destabilize Turkey. As for the death of Mehmet Sincar, it seemed that a shady Islamic extremist group known as Hezbollah ('The Party of God') was responsible.

It was true that factional in-fighting between Kurdish groups had always been rife. It was also true that scores of PKK supporters in the southeast had been murdered by an Islamic Hezbollah organization. But only a handful of Hezbollah had been arrested – was it really independent from the security forces, or were the security forces using the group to assassinate Kurdish activists?

At the local headquarters of the Islamic revivalist Refah ('Welfare') Party, it was clear that there were those prepared to kill Kurdish nationalists on religious grounds. 'If you insult religion there's bound to be a reaction,' said a party official, explaining that it was not 'good Islam' for the PKK to take women off into the mountains and train them as guerrillas.

An Islamic revival was taking place in Batman. Islamic bookshops in the town sold pamphlets with Ayatollah Khomeini on the cover and the proportion of women in purdah was high. Local religious leaders argued that Kurds were disillusioned with the PKK, the radical Kurdish MPs and the mainstream political parties in equal measure: radical Islam was filling the vacuum. An old man in Batman pulled off his hat to show me the gash in his skull, created he said by a thwack from a Turkish rifle: 'How can you expect me to like the state when they do this?' he asked.

At best the security forces had failed, perhaps wilfully, to stop inter-Kurdish violence in Batman; at worst the state was more directly involved. In 1995, a Turkish parliamentary commission investigating extra-judicial killings quoted Batman's deputy governor and police chief as saying that 'military units' were training Hezbollah militants. The commission confirmed that the PKK and Hezbollah carried out murders, but claimed that murderers were also being sheltered in security forces' accommodation. As for the Sincar case, the Turkish Justice Ministry said that Hezbollah militants were detained by police but had been acquitted for lack of evidence in November 1994.

At the end of my trip to Batman in 1993, I took my police escorts to lunch in a local restaurant. One of them tried to explain the situation by pulling the salt, pepper and toothpicks towards him and mapping out a triangle on the tablecloth.

'There's us, there's the PKK and there's the Hezbollah,' he said. 'The people in the middle are scared of all of us, frightened of us all.'

Mehmet Sincar continued to be the subject of controversy for some time after his death. His body was stranded in an Ankara hospital morgue for a week, as relatives argued with government officials over how the burial ceremony should be conducted. When mourners gathered outside the DEP party office in the Turkish capital they were severely beaten up by police – the scene was aired across the country on a commercial television channel.

'Since we started I have never been so confident,' Abdullah Öcalan told journalists in Lebanon. 'Then, nobody was talking about the Kurdish identity, but now they are. The war has reached the point of no return.'

The Turkish chief-of-staff General Güreş stepped up his rhetoric, too, promising that the rebels would be 'crushed' by next spring. It was announced that a special military team of up to 10,000 men was being trained to follow the rebels into the mountains. The soldiers would live like the PKK for up to six weeks at a stretch.

For the first time in almost a year, Turkish jets resumed bombing suspected PKK camps in the 'safe haven' of northern Iraq. Despite their earlier cooperation with the Turks, the Iraqi Kurds said they were furious, that there were no permanent PKK camps, just roving rebel units, and that Iraqi Kurdish civilians were again being killed by mistake.

The PKK bans journalists

In the autumn of 1993 the PKK proved its powers of intimidation within Turkey by banning journalists from visiting the southeast. Newspaper representatives in Diyarbakır were told that the 'bourgeois press . . . has become the spokesman of the state's dirty war'. Only the Diyarbakır office of the pro-Kurdish *Gündem* dared stay open, but the paper had trials of its own. *Gündem* representative Hasan Özgün, soon to end up in prison, told me he had not slept at home for months in case gunmen followed him there and killed him. The paper's owner was under arrest, and two *Gündem* streetsellers had been stabbed within the space of a few weeks.

During a foreign trip Prime Minister Çiller told prominent Turkish journalists that she was considering the 'Basque model' in Spain as a response to the Kurdish problem. But shortly afterwards Mrs Çiller denied saying any such thing; even if she had wanted to apply some political imagination to the Kurdish crisis, neither the hawkish parliament nor the military would apparently hear of it. Although President Demirel had spoken of a 'Kurdish reality' in 1991, most Turkish politicians dared not contemplate a break with the past: for the sake of national unity, the existence and rights of an ethnic Kurdish minority had to be denied.

The monastery of Mar Gabriel.

Turkey saw in the beginning of 1994 with a sharp rise in human rights violations by the security forces. The Turkish Human Rights Association reported that ten people, most of them Kurds, were tortured to death in January, while another eleven suspects went 'missing'. The figures matched half the total recorded for all of 1993.

Christians under fire

It was dawn on the feast day of Saint Simeon, and the monastery of Mar Gabriel in southeast Turkey was filled with singing; two rows of choirboys chanting hymns in Aramaic, the ancient language spoken by Jesus Christ. The music was bewildering and infused the gloom with a hypnotic sense of calm, while the tiny church windows glowed ever brighter with the sunrise.

Syriac Christians have been worshipping at Mar Gabriel for almost 1,600 years, since the monastery was founded in AD 397. But when the monks herded the cattle inside at dusk and the monastery gates were shut, the talk around the stove was of war. 'We don't know who is strong and who is weak,' said one monk, 'all we know is that it is getting worse.'

At the end of 1993 a bomb went off outside the monastery gates, killing a civilian driver. Then in January 1994 a local priest was held hostage, allegedly by 'Hezbollah' Islamic extremists. He was reported to have been buried up to his neck and hung upside down in chains during his four-day captivity. Soldiers and village guard militia had tortured Christian shepherds and emptied the Christian village of Hassana, while the PKK in turn killed Christians who accepted the village guard system.

Syriac religious leaders told me their situation had worsened since the regional governor of the southeast, Ünal Erkan, claimed that at least a hundred Armenians were fighting in the PKK's ranks. There are hardly any Armenians left in southeast Turkey, but the governor's words served as an invitation for Muslims in the southeast to turn against Christians, regardless of their ethnic background.

The town of Midyat near Mar Gabriel monastery was 90 per cent Syriac Christian in 1950, but only 10 per cent now. Over the years, thousands of Christians have fled to Germany, Sweden and the United States, so that there are fewer than a thousand Syriac families left in the windswept 'Tur Abdin' region of the southeast. 'My father left his fields, vineyards, everything,' said a 25-year-old pilgrim named Simeon. It was Simeon's birthday, and he told me he was visiting Mar Gabriel monastery in honour of the saint after whom he was named. His parents had been smuggled illegally into Germany as asylum-seekers; now Simeon was asking in his prayers whether he, too, should leave.

Kurdish MPs are arrested

In March 1994, six Kurdish nationalist MPs were arrested by police, after parliament voted to lift their immunity from prosecution. The move was backed by Mrs Çiller, who described the Kurds as 'PKK sheltering under the parliament's roof'. She condemned one Kurd, Hatip Dicle, as a traitor after he appeared to condone the killing of five Turkish army cadets in a PKK bombing outside Istanbul.

Apart from one independent deputy, Mahmut Alınak, the MPs were all members of the pro-Kurdish Democracy Party or DEP. The MPs were accused of receiving orders from the PKK and charged with treason for 'actions aimed at dividing the country'. One MP, Orhan Doğan, was said to have sheltered a wounded PKK guerrilla at his Ankara home. Turkish television showed Mr Doğan being manhandled by police as he was taken from parliament to prison. No one doubted that some of the MPs had PKK links. The half-brother of one was a PKK commander, the son of another was also with the rebels. But none stood accused of any acts of violence, and their arrest came as sad proof that a political solution to Turkey's Kurdish problem was unlikely as long as elected representatives were forbidden to speak.

'Why should the Turkish Government talk to criminals?' President Demirel responded when asked about the imprisoned MPs. He argued that if Turkey changed laws which limited freedom of expression and Kurdish cultural rights, that would deliver a propaganda victory to PKK separatists. 'No one should have the right to divide the country,' the President concluded.

In June 1994, another two DEP MPs were arrested while a further five fled to Belgium after the constitutional court in Ankara closed the party down. Turkey was spectacularly ignoring mounting criticism from abroad in order to rid itself of what it saw as a threat to national security.

New Year again

In case of trouble over the March 1994 Newroz, thousands of recruits were sent to bolster the estimated 150,000 Turkish troops in the 'emergency region'. There were searches and checkpoints every few miles, while tanks and armoured vehicles controlled the entrances to towns and remote mountain passes.

A PKK communiqué in the run-up to the New Year said the guerrillas would 'more than ever take the burden of active resistance'. It instructed Kurds to close their shops, wear national clothing and wait for orders. As our military convoy cruised through the darkness near the town of Silvan, we saw the silhouettes of Turkish soldiers waiting for action along the road, illuminated by a distant flash in the night sky.

In the town of Kulp, old men in a teahouse fell completely silent when we began to ask questions. 'If we speak, we are criminals,' one voice said eventually. 'We are trapped,' said another. The local English teacher standing behind us had been sent in by the police to report back everything that was said. Kulp's military commander, Ali Ergülmez, sounded trapped, too. 'My children are forced to stay inside all day,' he said. 'What kind of human rights is that?'

Islam wins

Not only was it the Kurdish Newroz, but municipal elections were being held across Turkey that week. The pro-Kurdish Democracy Party had pulled out of the poll after a bomb attack on the party headquarters and the arrest of some three hundred DEP members within the space of two months.

The PKK ordered a boycott of the elections, leaving Kurdish villagers confused as to how they should respond to the poll. 'Our Kurdish MPs have been locked up,' a villager explained, 'but if we don't vote, then twenty-four hours later the army will burn our houses down.'

In the event, more than 60 per cent of voters in the southeast were reported to have taken part in the elections – a victory against the PKK's intimidation campaign and an indication that, unlike the 1992 Newroz, the security forces now had the situation under control. The anticipated Kurdish uprising or 'serhildan' never happened. It was a victory, too, for the Islamic Welfare Party, which gained from the PKK/DEP boycott by winning seats across the southeast with promises of Muslim brotherhood between Turks and Kurds.

But election day was marred by violence across Turkey. Three foreign tourists

Regional elections in the southeast. Secular parties like Tansu Çiller's True Path Party (DYP) were abandoned in favour of the Islamic revivalist Welfare Party.

were injured in a Kurdish bomb blast outside the Hagia Sophia museum, one of Istanbul's most famous landmarks. In the southeastern province of Şırnak, around twenty civilians were reportedly killed when a Turkish aircraft bombed Kurdish villages. The Government explained that the settlements were occupied by the PKK but admitted that there may have been collateral damage.

Across the country, Mrs Çiller maintained a surprising level of national support. Despite the worst economic downturn in fifty years, the Prime Minister's tough line against the PKK and Kurdish nationalists in parliament had, apparently, earned her the admiration of the general public. That summer, parliament voted by 193 to 147 to extend for another six months the mandate of allied fighter jets protecting Kurds in northern Iraq. The result caused sighs of relief in London and Washington, where there was concern that their policy of keeping Iraq out in the cold was being undermined by the desire of many Turks to end the Kurdish 'safe haven' and return the region to President Saddam Hussein.

But Turkey's Foreign Minister, Hikmet Çetin, presented parliament with the uncomfortable truth that if Iraq's Kurds were not protected from the Iraqi regime, they could flee across the Turkish border as they had in 1991. And Mr Çetin admitted that Turkey's vital role in the 'safe haven' had both military and diplomatic spin-offs – by which he was thought to mean that Ankara could attack the PKK in northern Iraq with minimal international criticism.

The British on the beach

In June 1994 the first British tourist was killed and several were injured after PKK bombs were let off in the Marmaris and Fethiye coastal resorts. A Kurdish news agency in Germany with close PKK ties warned of more violence to come. 'If the Turks want to attack Kurdish villages, they must expect retaliation,' an agency spokesman said; 'There has been a call for civilians to take up arms.'

I found a suntanned British tourist sipping Bacardi and coke beside a swimming pool on the Marmaris waterfront. 'It comes up on the telly sometimes but I don't think people in Britain know anything about the Kurds,' he said, adamant that an isolated incident would not spoil his precious annual fortnight abroad. Other nationalities were more cautious; the media in Germany, Belgium and Scandinavian countries had given far more coverage to Turkey's Kurdish problem, and bookings from these countries were reported to be between 20 and 30 per cent down on the year before.

Turks in Marmaris told me defensively that they had been working alongside Kurdish shop owners and hoteliers all their lives. They pointed out that Turkey's

Refugees outside the town hall in Diyarbakır, waiting for food and clothing.

Foreign Minister was Kurdish, and that even the late President, Turgut Özal, claimed to have Kurdish blood. They saw the PKK problem as purely one of terrorism which would either be defeated or at least reduced to a containable level. The question of Kurdish education, Kurdish broadcasting or devolution for the Kurds was not on the agenda.

More talk of peace

In August 1994, Abdullah Öcalan again spoke of peace. 'The situation is suitable for a ceasefire,' the PKK leader said in a BBC interview marking the tenth anniversary of the group's armed uprising. 'A ceasefire is much more sensible than a meaningless and somewhat balanced fight.'

But the violence continued, with more than sixty people reported killed in the week following Öcalan's remarks. Although the PKK commander insisted in a newspaper interview later that year that 'Turkey's unity or sovereignty [was] not under threat', Ankara had no intention of negotiating with the country's most wanted terrorist.

The nationalistic Turkish press had been so sweetened by Government loans that it was scarcely in a position to question Ankara's handling of the crisis. And it was dangerous to probe too deeply; two television journalists, Erhan Akyıldız and Ali Tefvik Berber, were sentenced to two months' imprisonment for making a television programme on draft dodging. Although they were later acquitted upon appeal, it was the first time that reporters had been tried and sentenced by a military court since the 1980 military coup.

According to official figures, the cost of policing the southeast had risen from $US 4.4 billion for 1992 to 7.5 billion in 1993. The PKK conflict was therefore costing roughly 20 per cent of the national budget as well as feeding into Turkey's worsening image abroad. Yet Turkish political parties were too numerous and too nationalistic to offer a serious challenge to the military's handling of the crisis, and the general public was not crying out for a change of approach, either. It was true that draft resistance organizations had been set up, and even the chief-of-staff's son was accused of extending his time at drama school to postpone conscription.

But most Turks considered the southeast an honourable graveyard for the more than two thousand 'Mehmetçiks' (the Turkish equivalent of Tommies or GI Joes) who had died there since 1984. The message was driven home that the PKK had to be defeated, and that its attempts to build artificial barriers between Turks and Kurds would not succeed.

The rebels had killed so many school teachers in the southeast that, according to the education ministry, more than three thousand schools were forced to close in the 1993–94 academic year. Around a quarter of teachers assigned to the region in 1994 refused to take up their posts. Faced with this violence, the Turks were not going to make concessions on Kurdish rights, purely to curry favour abroad. Policy changes were far more likely to stem from the belief that the risk to national security had been eliminated. The battle to crush the PKK was still top priority, and would be waged at almost any cost.

An open secret – burning Kurdish villages

Salih Oğuz was one of about a thousand Kurdish refugees crowded around a padlocked warehouse beside the town hall in Diyarbakır in November 1994. Mr Oğuz was hoping that this might be his lucky day; he had brought a plastic bag along with him in case the town's pro-Islamic municipal council decided to give one of its free handouts of potatoes, cooking oil or second-hand clothes. While he was waiting, Mr Oğuz told me that until a few months earlier he had lived as a walnut farmer in the village of Akçabudak, northeast of Diyarbakır. 'The Turkish soldiers came and told us we were terrorists and that they wanted to burn the place,' he explained, claiming that the army had evacuated all two hundred houses. He pulled from his jacket pocket a copy of a letter about the incident which he had sent to the regional governor. 'All my friends and I are living in Diyarbakır now,' the letter read. 'There is no way we can support ourselves here, and we don't know what to do.'

By now the civilian exodus from southeast Turkey had become so great that it could no longer be hidden from view. In a rare burst of glasnost on the Kurdish problem, the Turkish press reported that more than five hundred Kurdish settlements had been emptied or destroyed so far that year. An influx of refugees was transforming the outskirts of Diyarbakır into a labyrinth of ugly shanty towns, swimming in mud. Concrete tower blocks had sprung up by the dozen to house thousands of new arrivals.

Villages and hamlets had undoubtedly been razed by the PKK, which according to human rights groups killed at least 350 prisoners and civilians during 1993 and 1994. But Kurds queuing for charity in Diyarbakır were adamant that Turkish soldiers were responsible for the large majority of cases, apparently operating a scorched earth policy intended to cut the PKK off from its supporters and potential recruits. 'The army used explosives, they burned everywhere,' said one Kurd from Yazkonak Shatos, a village of more than two hundred houses in Bingöl province allegedly destroyed by security forces in July 1994. He dismissed as nonsense a claim by Prime Minister Çiller that PKK rebels disguised in military clothing were responsible for such attacks.

In the small town of Hozat in Tunceli province, refugees were crammed into every spare building available, awaiting the arrival of food and prefabricated housing promised by the state before the winter snows arrived. Some forty rural settlements in Tunceli were reckoned to have been abandoned within the space of two months, displacing around five thousand people, while 40,000 troops were scouring the Tunceli countryside in pursuit of PKK rebels. Fighter jets and US-supplied Cobra helicopters bombed mountains and forests.

Kamer Genç, a moderate Kurd serving as an MP for the junior coalition partner the Social Democrats, told me up to 80 per cent of Tunceli's rural population had left their villages in the last two years. Mr Genç, who was also deputy speaker of the Turkish parliament, was compelled to go public on the issue after he received overwhelming evidence from his constituents that security forces were destroying their homes. 'I told our Prime Minister and President but they didn't believe that Turkish soldiers could do such things,' he said. 'When the houses of my voters are burned down, I can't remain indifferent.'

President Demirel ordered an investigation into Mr Genç's claims. But when Turkey's deputy Prime Minister tried visiting the destroyed villages for himself, he was turned back by soldiers. Although the Interior Minister made the outlandish claim that villagers were setting their own houses on fire to claim state compensation, the depopulation of the southeast was becoming an important domestic issue for the first time.

'In Tunceli it is the state which is evacuating and burning villages,' claimed Human Rights Minister Azimet Köylüoğlu, adding that Turkish security forces 'should avoid the psychology of burning and destroying during their relentless fight against terrorism'. Mr Köylüoğlu was sacked shortly afterwards.

Prime Minister Çiller promised financial aid for Kurdish villagers driven from their homes, but when a delegation from Tunceli told her that army helicopters were seen ferrying in troops to burn villages, she was unconvinced. To the amazement of her fellow MPs, the Prime Minister made the absurd claim that the PKK might have acquired helicopters by now – perhaps, she said, from Russia, Armenia or Afghanistan.

The Prime Minister said that 548 collective villages would be built, where Kurds could live in safety without having to migrate to the cities. She pointed out that it would be easier to provide health, education and protection for those Kurds who agreed to cooperate; but the policy was reminiscent of Saddam Hussein's collective village policy in northern Iraq and seemed to endorse the evacuation and destruction of Kurdish rural settlements.

I think, therefore I am a terrorist

At five past nine on a wet November morning in 1994, the Turkish capital Ankara was dotted with people observing their annual minute's silence for Mustafa Kemal Atatürk, who had died at five past nine 56 years before.

At half past nine that same wet morning, the trial of eight Kurdish MPs resumed. For many Turks there was a clear connection between the court case and the anniversary of the death of Turkey's most famous son. It was Atatürk who had moulded the ethnically diverse subjects of the Ottoman Empire into a new unitary state, and now Kurdish nationalists faced the prospect of being put behind bars for threatening to unravel Atatürk's achievements.

'These people [the MPs] made propaganda about transforming Turkey into some

Above School children in Ankara preparing to observe the annual one-minute silence for Mustafa Kemal Atatürk.

Below Mahmut Talı Öngören of the Turkish Human Rights Foundation.

kind of federation,' said Çoşkun Kırca, a former Turkish Ambassador to the United Nations who was unrepentant about the Kurds' trial. 'Propaganda against the unitary state is a crime.'

Ankara seemed fuller than ever of stern disciplinarians like Mr Kırca. The defenders of the Atatürk cult had become a dispirited lot, hypersensitive to criticism and not in the mood to be lectured by Western governments on the country's human rights practices. 'We are in our trenches,' a Turkish diplomat told me when I asked him what life in the Foreign Ministry was like.

Attempts by various branches of the state apparatus to stifle dissent had reached new and frightening levels of intensity. Mahmut Talı Öngören of Ankara's Human Rights Foundation told me his telephone was being tapped and that police were picking up torture victims for questioning as soon as they left the foundation's medical centre. More than 1,200 torture victims – the majority Kurdish – had been accepted for treatment between 1991 and 1994.

'The Kurdish problem has reached the point where if you say something in favour of Kurdish people, everybody says you support the PKK,' Mr Öngören said. His research showed that around eighty journalists, writers and academics had been given prison sentences in 1994, mainly for speeches and writings on the Kurdish issue, compared with eighteen in 1993.

'In Turkey we don't say "I think therefore I am". We say "I think, therefore I am a terrorist",' joked Haluk Gerger by telephone from prison. A former university academic and editor of *Özgür Gündem* – and like Mr Öngören an ethnic Turk – Mr Gerger was jailed for twenty months after he sent a fax to a political meeting which, when read out, was judged by police observers to be a criminal act.

By the end of 1994 the Social Democrats (SHP), junior partners in Mrs Çiller's coalition Government, had drafted an amendment to Turkey's anti-terror law which would make it more difficult for judges to sentence the likes of Mr Gerger for crimes of thought. But the SHP was weak, commanding less than 10 per cent in national opinion polls. Its perceived woolly liberalism in the face of the PKK threat meant that the anti-terror amendment was set to be blocked or significantly amended by parliament. 'It's all cosmetic,' said Mr Gerger. 'They are trying to gain time in Europe and the United States by saying they will release us, but Turkey isn't ready for change. You either shut up here or you go to prison.'

The Kurdish MPs go to jail

The most controversial court case in Turkey's recent legal history ended in December 1994, when six Kurdish MPs were awarded prison sentences of up to fifteen years. Another two were also sentenced, but released due to the time they had already served in jail. The verdicts fell short of the death penalty, but neverthe-less provoked outrage among the small army of European parliamentarians and human rights campaigners who filled the courtroom to overflowing.

The judge said in his summing up that five Kurdish MPs – Leyla Zana, Selim Sadak, Ahmet Türk, Orhan Doğan and Hatip Dicle – had made speeches in favour of the PKK. According to articles 168 and 169 of the Turkish penal code, which outlaw helping terrorists or associating with them, the five were each sentenced to fifteen years. Another MP, Sedat Yurtaş, was given seven and a half years for sup-porting the rebels. 'This is not justice!' exploded one of the deputies, who had to be restrained as Turkish soldiers led the group from the dock. Relatives in the packed gallery hollered Kurdish battlecries, ignoring Turkish policemen guarding every aisle.

Yusuf Alataş, head of more than two hundred lawyers defending the Kurds, said he had repeatedly been denied the chance to introduce evidence and witnesses. The court heard instead from a 452-page indictment which included information based on the MPs' tapped telephone calls, and confessions obtained from impris-oned PKK rebels. The Kurds dismissed both as fabrications and lies. At one stage it was claimed that four of the MPs had gone into the mountains of southeast Turkey to visit a PKK camp. But the Kurds said they were on holiday at the time and that,

The court building in Ankara where Kurdish MPs were on trial in November 1994.

as they were always followed by police, the accusation was ridiculous.

Several newspapers commented that the decision was bad news. 'Unless the discrepancy between Turkish laws and universal democratic laws is removed,' said the left-wing daily *Cumhuriyet*, 'Turkey will find everything more difficult . . . we face being shunned by the West if we fail to close the political gap between us.' In the same month Turkey's most radical Kurdish newspaper received a near-mortal blow. Bombs destroyed both the Istanbul and Ankara offices of *Özgür Ülke* (Free Country), which had replaced *Gündem* after it was banned earlier in the year. One person was killed and more than twenty injured.

President Demirel condemned the bombings and promised that the Government would investigate. 'We have no doubt that it was the state that did this,' Baki Karadeniz, the paper's editor, said afterwards. 'They have accused us of being separatists who want to destroy Turkey. This is a natural outcome of their attempts to silence us.'

The throttling of free speech

Yaşar Kemal, the only Turkish author to have been nominated for the Nobel Prize for Literature, became the most distinguished writer to suffer from the atmosphere of growing intolerance on the Kurdish issue. In May 1995, the 71-year-old Kurdish-born novelist was taken to court to face charges of threatening state unity because he had written in a German magazine about his vehement opposition to Turkey's war with the PKK.

'Weren't thousands of villages burnt down?' Kemal asked the court. 'Wasn't the dignity of a whole nation trampled on? Is it forgivable, what we have done?' But the author insisted that Turks and Kurds should not live apart from one another. Turkey is a 'garden of a thousand flowers and colours', Yaşar Kemal said. 'I don't want one flower to go missing from that garden.' Then the judge dictated to his typist a summary of what the accused had said: 'My real concern is what is going to happen if this war . . . makes it difficult for people to live together. It should be brought to an end before it causes irreversible damage.'

When Kani Yılmaz, a PKK representative, was arrested in London in 1994 protesters
gathered outside the Home Office.

Chapter 4

Atatürk's children

In March 1995, Roger Hutchings and I revisited the Kurdish town of Cizre to watch the population usher in their traditional 'Newroz' or New Year. Once they had disembarked from buses and tractor trailers ferrying them in from outlying villages, hundreds of Kurds walked in spring sunshine down Cizre high street, awkwardly waving Turkish flags in front of police marksmen. A plainclothes policeman filmed the scene from the turret of a bullet-proof Land Rover. Whenever the video camera was turned on, the crowd responded by bursting into polite rounds of applause.

This Newroz was peaceful, unlike three years earlier when I had seen a very different demonstration, walking down the same street. Back in 1992, Kurds shouted 'Kurdistan!' and there were shootings and deaths. Nowadays you must look among the hundreds of thousands of Kurds living in Europe for such violent outbursts of Kurdish nationalism; in the ancient Kurdish homeland, the flame of rebellion is flickering weakly, for the time being at least.

The Turks have succeeded, not by winning Kurdish hearts and minds, but by pouring in arms, men and informers – by killing, arresting or imprisoning tens of thousands of PKK members, suspects and supporters. After more than a decade of conflict, the PKK's powerbase in rural communities of the southeast is vanishing. More than half the 60,000 Kurds of Cizre are reckoned to have left in the last three years.

According to Amnesty International, there has been a steady rise in the number of people shot dead on the streets of the southeast – over 20 in 1991, rising to 362 in 1992, over 400 in 1993 and 380 by November 1994. In most cases, the relatives of the dead believed they were killed for political reasons by agents of the state. Human rights abuses are committed all across Turkey, and not solely against Kurds. But in the southeast an atmosphere of such secrecy and fear has been established that torture, murder and the torching of civilian settlements can be committed there with almost complete impunity. Short of imposing martial law, there is not much more that Turkey can do to silence its critics in the southeast.

Military operations have continued beyond Turkey's borders. In March 1995, 35,000 Turkish troops crossed into northern Iraq. Prime Minister Çiller billed the operation as even bigger than Turkey's invasion of Cyprus in 1974 and said that more than five hundred PKK rebels were killed. Iraqi Kurdish leaders disputed that figure and claimed that it would be impossible to eradicate small and highly mobile PKK units hiding in the mountains along the border.

Germany responded to the invasion by suspending arms sales to Turkey, while the rest of Ankara's allies demanded the withdrawal of her troops from the 'safe haven'. Their underlying concern was Turkey's failure to tackle Kurdish grievances, primarily human rights abuses, which helped fuel the PKK's rise in the first place.

Western foreign policy towards Turkey has generally been something of a carrot and stick affair – encouraging the country's westward orientation, but rarely according this once great Ottoman power the political importance and social acceptance it seeks. The country's long-standing bid for European Union membership has been put on hold by Brussels, but Turkey has been earmarked as one of the world's top ten emerging markets by the Clinton administration, and in December 1995 the European Parliament overcame its misgivings over human rights to admit Ankara into a customs union, beginning in 1996. Both Brussels and Washington believe that Turkey should be more firmly anchored within the west, particularly at a time when the state's failure to improve living standards is increasing the appeal of Islamic revivalism.

There is also no lack of international condemnation for the PKK. In November 1993, France and Germany banned the group after two waves of Kurdish attacks on Turkish property in 28 cities across Europe. Kurdish gunmen occupied the Turkish Consulate in Munich and threatened to shoot their hostages unless Chancellor Helmut Kohl denounced Turkey's war in the southeast. Mr Kohl did not oblige, and after fourteen hours of negotiation the Kurds surrendered.

But condemnation for the PKK does not apparently make it any easier for Ankara to admit to its friends that it has a Kurdish problem beyond terrorism. Many Turkish politicians refuse to acknowledge a connection between PKK terror and official policies which have long denied Kurdish rights.

If Turkey's Kurds are to receive any significant degree of cultural and political rights, Atatürk's children will have to unlearn some of the worst dogmatic excesses of the past. Much of Atatürk's militaristic legacy has already lost its grip on Turkish national life; the economy is gradually throwing off the shackles of state ownership and opening itself up to the outside world, and Islam has come out of the closet where Atatürk kept it, so much so that Islamic revivalist politicians now challenge the secular system of government. Yet on the issue of recognizing and allowing for ethnic diversity, Turkey has shown the least inclination to change.

The country's late president, Turgut Özal, realized that the authoritarianism of Atatürk and his heirs had to be tempered by a degree of reform. Mr Özal started by

At their annual cultural festival (essentially a PKK rally) near Maastricht in Holland, Kurds stand
in front of a mural of a Kurdish youth killed by the German police.

unbanning the Kurdish language, even claiming that his grandmother was of
Kurdish origin. But with Özal's death in 1993, the possibility of curtailing the PKK
conflict by political means receded. Instead, Ankara has mismanaged its Kurdish
rebellion and damaged its democracy by clamping down on all forms of dissent.
Such a self-defeating policy can only exacerbate Kurdish grievances in the future.

The fear in parliament – indeed across Turkish society – is understandable.
Dogged by Islamic revivalism and PKK violence, and with high inflation and
unemployment threatening to provoke social unrest, many Turks do not feel ready
for fuller democracy or giving Kurds more rights. They are frightened that Turkey's
ethnic mosaic will not be able to withstand the strain of competing social-interest
groups and that the country will fall apart. Less than eighty years on from the
foundation of the republic, the Turks do not yet trust themselves.

Turkey's fears for its future have been aggravated by ethnic and nationalist conflicts in the former Yugoslavia and across the post-Soviet Caucasus, and above all by the establishment of an autonomous Kurdish zone in northern Iraq. Many Turks believe that unless they defend Atatürk's nationalist ideology, coined during the Communist era and influenced by Nazi Germany, then Atatürk's sacred borders will begin to crack.

The country is stuck in a Catch-22 situation which is pushing the Turks' faith in democracy to the limit. Abolishing undemocratic laws and practices could be the thin end of the wedge, running the risk of intensifying the PKK's struggle for an independent Kurdish state; yet if Turkey does not fulfil the expectations of its Western allies it risks being ostracized, and that in turn will encourage disillusioned Turks to seek political solace in revivalist Islam.

After three military interventions in the last forty years (1960, 1971 and 1980), Turkey has a tradition of coups, a tendency to resolve its problems through force. Civilian governments have yet to prove that this time they have more than military answers and outmoded ideology to deal with the PKK threat. That will require flexibility and imagination from Turkey's politicians, who will need to be strong enough to shape public opinion with new and more liberal interpretations of what it means to be a Turkish citizen.

So far PKK bomb attacks in major Turkish cities have been sporadic, probably because the rebels realize how little support there would be for an all-out Turkish–Kurdish war; but if the PKK's attempts to 'liberate' Kurdistan were accompanied by frequent bombings and assassinations in Istanbul, Ankara and elsewhere, polarization between Turkish and Kurdish nationalists could reach dangerous levels.

In the last few years the war with the PKK has driven a vast Kurdish underclass into western Turkey in search of work; whatever the success of the security forces in the southeast, migrant ghettos in the west are becoming hot-beds of social unrest. Some 20,000 Kurds are thought to be arriving in the southwestern province of Adana every month. Poverty and regular police intimidation there (including a high rate of torture) have turned derelict suburbs into ideal recruitment grounds for the PKK and other disillusioned malcontents.

'The soldiers are burning our villages, and here we are constantly being harassed by police,' commented a young Kurd in Istanbul during rioting in March 1995. Kurdish grievances in poor areas of Turkey's largest city undoubtedly helped fuel four days of violence in which at least 23 people were killed by police. Few in Turkey like contemplating yet another military coup, but the last one in 1980 was widely welcomed as a solution to the political violence plaguing the cities. Unless steps are taken to reduce Kurdish grievances, Turkey may once again be heading towards a level of violence which will prompt military intervention.

Busts and portraits of Atatürk can be seen all over Turkey, reminding Turks of the great man's achievements in creating a unitary, secular state. In the southeast, Atatürk's slogans of 'Motherland First' and 'Happy is the man who calls himself a Turk' are marked out in stones on barren hillsides for every passing shepherd, soldier or PKK rebel to see. Although embittered Kurds find such sentiments hard to swallow, that does not necessarily mean they want the PKK alternative of a Marxist-Leninist utopia. Most would probably settle for curbs on the behaviour of the security forces, rcognition of minority rights (education and broadcasting in Kurdish) and the acceptance of explicitly Kurdish political parties within the Turkish parliamentary system. It is only through democracy that a moderate Kurdish leadership will be able to develop as an alternative to the PKK.

Fostering better relations with hostile neighbours which harbour the PKK won't solve the Kurdish problem entirely – the group is firmly entrenched within Turkey. More investment in the southeast won't solve the Kurdish problem on its own, either, because the natural drain of migrants from a social and economic backwater is bound to continue.

Giving Turkey's Kurds an independent state is both impractical and for the time being unthinkable, given the area's economic dependence on the rest of Turkey and the turmoil that would be caused if the borders of the Middle East were to

A Kurdish village in the mountains near Van.

be redrawn. Most Turks cannot even contemplate a Kurdish state because the country's current borders were dearly bought in a historic liberation war less than eighty years ago. And if Turkey were to abrogate its responsibilities towards the southeast, the lack of political structures and alternatives in what is still a tribal society would probably result in a regional bloodbath.

What is required (and what Turkey's Kurds surely deserve) is some form of recognition, so that they are no longer the most culturally repressed Kurdish population in the Middle East. The British analyst Andrew Mango has suggested the reintroduction of Kurdish place-names and the use of Kurdish as a second official language in local government and the courts. A degree of autonomy in Kurdish areas might one day be possible, if presented to the Turkish people as part of a package of reforms applied to local administrations across the country. Instead of dispatching governors from Ankara, more power could be devolved to regional councils.

In July 1995, Prime Minister Tansu Çiller steered through parliament a plan recommending devolution nationwide, in an attempt she said to make government more accountable to every Turkish citizen. Under pressure from Europe, the Turkish parliament also softened the terms of a law prohibiting freedom of expression. A court dropped its infamous legal action against the writer Yaşar Kemal, and two out of six Kurdish MPs jailed in 1991 were set free due to insufficient evidence that they were engaged in separatist activities.

More open discussion of the Kurdish problem in national newspapers and on television chat shows suggests that the debate in Turkish society is entering a more critically enlightened phase. But although the development of mass media will make it increasingly difficult to maintain a tradition of denial, it has been the primary task of this book to show how the Turkish state still seeks to solve the Kurdish problem – and assert its own power – by brutally suppressing dissent.

Select bibliography

Two books in Turkish document the rise of the PKK: *Kürt Dosyası* by the late Uğur Mumcu (Tekin Yayınevi, 1994) and *Apo ve PKK* by Mehmet Ali Birand (Milliyet Yayınları, 1992).

Books in English

Imset, Ismet G. *The PKK – a report on separatist violence in Turkey (1973–1992)* (Turkish Daily News Publications, Ankara, 1992).

McDowall, David *The Kurds: a nation denied* (Minority Rights Publications, London 1992).

McDowall, David *A modern history of the Kurds* (I.B. Tauris, London, 1995).

Mango, Andrew *Turkey – the challenge of a new role* (Centre for Strategic and International Studies, Washington, 1994).

Robins, Philip *Turkey and the Middle East* (Royal Institute of International Affairs, London, 1991).

van Bruinessen, Martin *Agha, Shaikh and State. The Social and Political Structures of Kurdistan* (reprinted by Zed Books, London, 1992).

Voices from the Crossfire

Atatürk let people speak their own language, then after the Treaty of Lausanne in 1923, everything changed. From then on, the Kurds couldn't talk about their identity. President Demirel still hasn't given us Kurdish education or television or cultural rights. What kind of admission of our existence is that? War achieves nothing. The Kurdish people have rebelled 28 times but each time they didn't achieve anything. But the PKK are our people, our children. They don't come from outer space. If Turkey gives us more rights, maybe the violence will stop. These rights won't be for the PKK, but for the Kurdish people. If the Turkish Government introduces some rights for the Kurds, this problem can be solved through politics, not in the mountains. I would like to live with Turkish people on equal terms. If we Kurds had this, I don't know what I would say about an independent state.

Leyla Zana, Kurdish MP, imprisoned in December 1994 and winner in 1995
of the European Parliament's Sakharov Prize

I haven't been home for a year because it is too dangerous. I stay in my office or with friends. According to the Government, anybody who wants to write about the Kurdish problem is a terrorist. They brand Kurdish people in the villages the same way. The Government thinks the PKK are like fish in the sea and the government wants to drain the water away. But it can never happen, they can never drain the water. Because we Kurds here, we are all in the water with the PKK. The guerrillas are the voice of the people.

journalist in Batman, southeast Turkey (1993)

It is impossible that the Government would burn the villagers' houses down – it is the PKK which forces people to leave. If terrorists come to live in empty villages, then of course we will destroy those villages. If villagers give food to terrorists, nothing will happen to them because it is not their fault. If I was a villager and a PKK terrorist asked me for food, I would probably give him a glass of whisky.

Government official, Diyarbakır (1994)

The majority of the Western press makes a radically false analysis of Turkey. They talk to the so-called intellectual class which is about as representative of public opinion here as Jean-Paul Sartre was in France. There will never be 'cultural rights' [for the Kurds] because a huge majority of the Turkish people don't want that. There are seven different forms of Kurdish 'patois'. The biggest, Kurmanji, only has 3,000 words. It is not a civilized language. We don't recognize the existence of ethnic minorities on our soil. Socialists say that expressing your thoughts shouldn't be a crime. But if there is a verbal attack tantamount to terrorist propaganda, I will not accept that. If a way of thinking provokes a physical attack then I am against it. Propaganda against the unitary state is a crime.

Çoşkun Kırca, right-wing MP and former Turkish Ambassador to
NATO and the United Nations (1994)

We have a prisoner here who is a very good cook. He is serving a ten-year sentence for insulting a former president of Turkey. In this country we don't say 'I think, therefore I am' but 'I think, therefore I am a terrorist'. When you close all the democratic channels, then inevitably you have violence. The Kurds can't express themselves freely, so you get the guerrillas. You either shut up here or you go to prison. But then again, the Government doesn't want us intellectuals in prison because it creates a headache for them in Europe and the United States. In every Kurdish family you will find a son or daughter wounded or killed with a bullet produced in the West. Whatever Western governments are doing on behalf of democratization in Turkey does not eradicate the West's guilt.

Haluk Gerger, former Associate Professor at Ankara University, imprisoned 1994

Tunceli is a wild place, favourable to terrorist activities. If the PKK wants to make a raid on a small village, it is very easy. People say the soldiers are burning down the villages, but when I talk to civil servants they say you cannot assume that a hundred per cent of the burnings is by one side or the other. The PKK is acting against the interests of Kurdish people. But some villages have been burned down and evacuated by soldiers, and this is barbarism. Some of the soldiers may think that if they destroy these villages it will be more difficult for the PKK to operate in the area. Approximately 80 per cent of the Tunceli population has left in the last two years. I can't go and see the villages myself because I can't travel freely.

Kamer Genç, MP for Tunceli and Deputy Speaker of the Turkish Parliament (1994)

The village of Akçabudak had two hundred houses. But in the spring [1994] soldiers came to the village and said there were terrorists and that they wanted to burn it. We escaped, because if we had stayed they would have killed us. It was true that the PKK came to our village. They took our food and then disappeared. We called them terrorists. The soldiers took food from us, too.

refugee in Diyarbakır, southeast Turkey

There were 250 to 300 houses in Yazkonak Shatos village. We grew apples, tomatoes, walnuts, wheat. We had a school but no teacher because he was too frightened to come. The soldiers said terrorists were going there. In July [1994] the soldiers burned everywhere. They used explosives, and in one minute all the houses came down. On the same day the regional governor came and he gave money to thirty families.

refugee in Diyarbakır, southeast Turkey

Refugees on their way to Diyarbakır.

When the PKK terror started the village of Alacıköy didn't take sides. But in September [1993] the security forces came and set all the houses and our tobacco alight. They came with planes and helicopters and set sixty or seventy houses alight. My eight cows were killed within two hours. The soldiers made the cows lie down and cut off their heads. All the men had escaped beforehand. They knew they couldn't do anything, and that if they stayed they would be taken away. Eleven men who did stay were taken away in a military helicopter. We haven't heard any news about them. I was hiding in a tree with my daughter and saw it with my own eyes. There were no terrorists there, but there was a forest nearby and the security forces probably thought it was a PKK camp, so they burned everything down without asking any questions. We were just living an ordinary life. The governor will probably say I am a terrorist, but I am just a farmer. We were all farmers. I don't have a job or any money, and we have eleven people living in our house.

refugee in Diyarbakır, southeast Turkey

We escaped here because we were afraid of the security forces, but some people joined the outside people in the mountains. They knew that if they stayed in the village they would be killed, so they escaped to the mountains. Probably the Turkish police want to move people from this part of Turkey so there won't be any Kurdish problem. I was beaten for nine days because they thought I let PKK terrorists stay in my home. But I told them that nothing like that happened. We have lived with Turkish people under the Turkish flag for many years so we don't want any other state; we are all Muslims together. If we had a Kurdish state, we would get the same torture and bad conditions that Turkey gives us.

refugee in Diyarbakır, southeast Turkey

If we go back to our village, we can feed our animals and look after our families. The Government may allow us to go back, provided that we work for them as village guards. But if we accept this the PKK terrorists will attack us, and if we don't accept then the security forces will attack us. We just want the terrorists and the security forces to leave us alone. We just want to live a decent life.

refugee in Diyarbakır, southeast Turkey

The PKK aims to establish a Kurdish government or state, but they kill Kurdish people and I can't understand the reason for that. We don't know what to do: we are caught between two forces and either one or the other attacks us. I hope people in Europe know what happens here, but I don't think they know how poor we are, how harsh life is, how we don't have anything to eat or wear.

refugee in Diyarbakır, southeast Turkey

We are a family of musicians. We left the town of Lice in 1993 and now we live in Diyarbakır. All the people have come to Diyarbakır. There was fighting for three days in Lice, so we hid where we keep our animals. Afterwards the soldiers wanted to burn our houses. They took everybody outside their houses and destroyed part of the town. Thousands have left Lice. We are scared of both sides, caught between two stones. We are too afraid to go back.

refugee in Diyarbakır, southeast Turkey

On the last day of school I was going home. I had just given my students their diplomas when two people attacked me with a knife. It was ten o'clock in the morning in the centre of Diyarbakır. The wound was seven centimetres deep. More than thirty teachers have been attacked in Diyarbakır since 1991 and only three or four survived. The PKK doesn't want teachers to come here and they kill people working for the Government. But the other side kills journalists, doctors and teachers too. Everyone knows I am a Kurdish nationalist. I believe the Government is guilty. Their aim is to push all educated people out of this part of Turkey. It is very easy to solve the Kurdish problem. The Government has to give Kurds the same rights as Turks – cultural and political rights. A better solution would be federation or autonomy, but independence would be best of all. Giving us Kurdish television and radio won't solve anything on its own. It's not enough.

teacher in Diyarbakır, southeast Turkey

I am Armenian. I married in 1914. My husband was killed in 1919 when an electric cable collapsed on to the street and electrocuted him. One day my father went to buy some meat for a kebab. My mother waited for him but he didn't come back; soldiers took him to prison. In those days, they were hanging Armenians from the trees and killing them. They killed my father along with many Armenians. My mother told me this when I was a baby. She wanted to send me to a Muslim school when I was a child. When I went there I said

Lüsiye Işçi, Armenian woman in Diyarbakır.

something in Armenian and they beat me so I never went back. Muslims in Diyarbakır want me to leave here, but I go to the Government and they give me help. Two months ago, some Muslims killed a man looking after the Armenian church. I closed my mouth. I didn't say anything. Six years ago there were twenty or thirty Armenian families in Diyarbakır and a priest in the church. Not now.

Lüsiye Işçı, one of the last surviving Armenians in Diyarbakır, southeast Turkey

There are fifty thousand displaced villagers in Diyarbakır who are not registered to vote, and more than a million across the southeast. Their houses have been burned down so they have had to migrate. We believe from very trustworthy sources that the security forces are doing it. Eighteen hundred villages have been burned down, mostly since 1993.

pro-Islamic Welfare Party official, Diyarbakır, southeast Turkey (1994)

We have around a thousand people in our village. We are protected by 53 village guards, armed with rifles and kalashnikovs. We don't do this village guard job for money, but to stop the terror organization which kills women and children. We are trained here in the village, and we are all volunteers who want to stop the PKK from entering the village.

Some of the PKK terrorists are from a neighbouring village and we know them. Sometimes we have to fight them. In the past they have taken our women into the mountains, they have brainwashed and kidnapped many people. They want people to do their national service in the PKK and not in the Turkish army.

The PKK brainwashed me and some of my friends. I loved adventure in the mountains and so I joined the PKK. I was 14 at the time. But then I saw that the PKK uses ignorant Kurdish people to smuggle heroin and make propaganda against the Turkish republic. They kill people, they take women to the mountains, they violate human rights. So after one month I went back home. When I surrendered to the security forces, the PKK attacked my family's home. If the PKK works on behalf of Kurdish people, why did they attack my house?

extracts from interviews with villagers in Ziyaret, near Ergani, southeast Turkey

When they took me to court for my writing I never expected such a childish thing to happen. They acted as if I had thrown an atom bomb. Even my fellow writers and friends cursed me, accusing Yaşar Kemal of swearing at the nation. My mission is to write novels so why should I endanger myself by saying such things? Well, I can't stay silent any longer. I have to speak, I want the bloodshed to stop. It is a great lie to say that Turkey is a democracy when we don't give 15 million Kurdish people their rights. Kurdish is one of the richest languages, but without a written literature, Kurdish will not prosper. There should be

Yaşar Kemal: the famous writer at home, he was put on trial after writing about the Kurdish issue.

Kurdish schools, but they won't let them have their own television channel, let alone a school. If Kurdish culture was allowed to exist, it would be so colourful, so rich. The Turkish state has been racist for the last seventy years. It is a disgrace to Turkey, to the West and to the whole world. But there won't be a civil war here between Turks and Kurds because we have been living together for a thousand years. I am Kurdish, but I think and write in Turkish.

Yaşar Kemal, Turkish author, on trial for separatist propaganda (1995)

Last week the Turks had an operation here. They herded up 2,000 people, and took away 25 for questioning. The PKK is a symbol of our freedom here. Yes, they burn schools, but the schools are teaching our children Turkish nationalist ideas. We don't want our children growing up to become our enemies.

man in Bismil, southeast Turkey

The government thinks our party is an extension of the PKK. We are both defending victims of the Turkish state but otherwise we are different. We are legal; the PKK has chosen an illegal path. Our purpose is to discuss openly the war that is being waged against the Kurdish people. But the lawmakers don't want democracy, they are afraid of it. In a real democracy, they would have to give all ethnic groups their rights. They say we want to divide the country but that is not our purpose. We want to give people the opportunity to live in freedom and equality.

spokesman for the banned pro-Kurdish Democracy Party, Istanbul

The PKK cannot be eliminated by burning down Kurdish villages. The PKK does not create events; events create the PKK. When people move from the southeast, the problem does not come to an end. On the contrary, the PKK gets stronger because of the feelings of those who are forced to leave their lands. We do not have any organic bond with the PKK, but the PKK gets its power from Kurdish people, and we get our political power from the people as well. There is no need for the Government to talk to the PKK; they should talk to the Kurdish MPs and Kurdish people. But members of our party are killed because some powers within the Government cannot tolerate the improvement of democracy in Turkey.

Selim Sadak, former pro-Kurdish Democracy Party MP, imprisoned 1994

In east and southeastern Turkey, it is difficult for the young to find work. Land is limited, the climate is harsh. It is sometimes difficult for them to get to universities and they become vulnerable. That is the basic issue. We tried in the past to create employment, but thirty economic plans have collapsed; because of lack of personnel, sometimes lack of capital. If you send teachers, they resign; if you send a professor to a university, he will not go. In any case, you cannot keep people on the land any more. These people see the world on 18-channel television, and they move to the big cities. Istanbul increases by 300,000 people every year, and I think 40 per cent of the population is from the east or southeast. People can express themselves in Kurdish and there are no ethnic barriers: we are united by living in this country and sharing the same religion. No single person can pretend to be of pure blood from one or other ethnic group.

Kamuran Inan, Kurdish-born MP, former government minister
and candidate for the Turkish presidency in 1993

We tried to take a different view from Turkish newspapers, but of course we had some difficulties. Seventeen of our workers were killed. If you write about a burning village or the bombing of the mountains, this is considered a separatist activity. We can't just disregard the PKK issue, they have got about 10,000 militants in the mountains. The war has reached an unbearable state for Turkish and Kurdish people. Twenty or thirty people are being killed every day. The expense is also beyond comprehension, Turkey can't afford it. The PKK wants to show that it is not just the southeast being hit by the war – the whole of Turkey could be hit. The PKK is a mass movement and cannot be ended by military operations alone. The movement will exist as long as the Kurdish people exist and as long as the political conditions which created the PKK remain.

Gülten Kişanak, managing editor, Özgür Gündem

Turkey is a nationalistic country, and public opinion is even tougher against the PKK than the military. The public don't want to hear of anything called concessions as far as the Kurds are concerned. But the Government has to do something and can't rely on the army hawks. The politicians know they cannot solve the Kurdish problem by military means alone. The problem is that we feel vulnerable; we think that if we give in to the Kurds, then the Laz or the Alevis or ethnic Georgians will start asking for things. Turkey is an ethnic mosaic, and the example of what happened in Yugoslavia has really frightened us. When it comes to defending the country, then everything else – democracy, human rights – disappears from the agenda. I think we have reached the peak of this conflict and that the PKK is going to change. It will see that it can't do anything with its armed struggle and it will set up its own political party. If we try to solve the Kurdish problem only by military means, then in the long run we are going to lose; but if we can convince the Kurds to give up the military struggle, and if we really give them the option of trying to get what they want by political means, then in the long run we are going to win.

Mehmet Ali Birand, leading Turkish journalist, Istanbul

Questions and answers with President Süleyman Demirel

There is no Kurdish problem in Turkey; there is terrorism. I think we are taking care of terrorism, everything is under control. I don't think terrorism will be the biggest problem in Turkey this year [1994]. It will drop somewhere down the agenda.

Under what circumstances do you think that the security forces have the right to destroy and evacuate villages?

State security forces would not burn Turkish villages. There is no logic to it. They are Turkish villages, no matter who lives in them. But there is fighting. If there is a fight between the security forces and the criminals, and if something happens to the houses, I don't think you can say that village was burned by the security forces. That place is no longer a village; it is a place where criminals are located.

If you break the law by making a speech which 'threatens the unity of the Turkish state', don't you think it is time the law changed?

No, I don't think so. No one should have the right to divide the country. Democracy should not allow the division of the country. Turkey is not ready for that. England may be, but not Turkey. I don't think Turkey should be blamed for wanting to stay a unitary state.

Don't you think that democratic measures would help Kurds feel more a part of this country and help reduce the PKK problem?

You've got to be very careful here. If the killers get a prize for killing, then they will kill some more. We never give moral support to killers, but if there is anyone who says, 'I am a Kurd, I am a first-class citizen of Turkey but I need this and that,' then we will consider it. They already have a hundred representatives in parliament.

Why don't you allow Kurdish broadcasting, Kurdish education in schools?

Why should I do that? If we do that, the PKK will be rewarded. It will say that it wants autonomy; then a flag; then a state. For the time being, Turkey has to protect her unity. You have to learn how to live under one flag. I don't think that democracy and human rights mean that you should just divide your country. If it comes to that, it is not democracy.

extracts from interview with President Süleyman Demirel, 1994

•   •   •

You can't say that all murders are political killings. Some are revenge killings, committed for reasons very much related to the feudal structure pervasive in the region. In most cases the relatives of the dead person don't help us; they withhold the name of the killer. Maybe people don't help because they are afraid of terrorists. The Hezbollah organization chooses a remote place, approaches a victim, shoots once or twice and disappears into the back-streets. The PKK kills people who want to leave the PKK on the grounds that they know inside information. At one point the PKK and Hezbollah tried to destroy one another.

Bekir Selçuk, chief prosecutor, southeast Turkey

Approximately 98 per cent of the people killed by unidentified persons have served prison sentences or were thought to be supporters of the PKK. We do not believe that the PKK has any reason to kill them. There is a 'Hezbollah' here, not like the one in Lebanon, but established by the state. We can show you some of the killers walking down the street in Diyarbakır when they should be in jail. Just four days ago an accountant friend of mine was killed just seventy metres away from a police station. When the murders started I was like a lunatic, walking down the street cautiously, like an animal. I'm afraid of only one thing: that I will die early.

member of Human Rights Association, Diyarbakır

A PKK informer gave my name to police. According to his testimony, we lawyers were working as PKK couriers, carrying cigarettes, pens and even cyanide to people in prison. It is impossible to do this because when lawyers go into prison and come out again, they are searched thoroughly. The prisoners are searched, too. There's just no evidence for it. I personally think I was detained because I work for the Human Rights Association. I was arrested right outside the court. I was put inside a car and blindfolded. Because I could not and would not answer their questions, their best bet was torture. After ten minutes of argument, I took my dress off. If I had not got undressed, they would have done it themselves. They soaked me three times in freezing water. Jets of water crashed onto my body from all sides. The first time I fainted. I was kicked and beaten. As a lawyer, how can I sign a confession without having read it? But you don't have any choice. I asked them why they had blindfolded me and they said it was forbidden to talk, to ask questions or answer questions. They said that either I had to sign the confession or be taken to another place for torture. In the end they gave up. I told them I wouldn't sign it, and they told me to go to the prosecutor's office if I wanted to make a complaint. Even if you are a lawyer, you cannot do anything. The prosecutors believe the word of the security forces. A doctor won't give you a medical report stating that you have been tortured.

lawyer, southeast Turkey

First of all the security forces should not attack villages and burn our houses down. Up in the mountains there are no villages left. The only authority that makes any decisions around here is the army. Secondly, we need some factories because unemployment is very high here. But a safe life is far more important to us than the economy. What is the point of having a healthy economy if people are being shot dead on the street?

Turkish culture and Kurdish culture have intermingled over the years and we have become assimilated, but Kurdish people do have distinct characteristics. There is our language. Education in the Kurdish language is not possible. Why can't I watch television in my mother tongue, or read papers written in Kurdish, or educate my children in Kurdish? In order to preserve our culture, we must have our identity recognized.

men in a teahouse in Diyarbakır, southeast Turkey

An interview with Kani Yılmaz, chief spokesman in Europe for the PKK (1994)

What is the PKK fighting for?

We want a free Kurdish nation. We don't mean separatism between Turkish and Kurdish nations but we insist on independence. We have said from time to time that we are ready to sit down and talk, to consider any alternatives – even federation.

Kurds listening to Kani Yılmaz (right) at a Kurdish festival near Maastricht.

Turkish intelligence says there are around 10,000 PKK guerrillas. What's your estimate?

There are over 35,000 guerrillas out there. We have twelve training camps in Turkish-occupied Kurdistan. We stopped using a training camp in Lebanon. We don't use Iran.

You are fighting the second largest army in NATO and you say you are winning. How do you expect me to believe you?

In 1984 we started off with two hundred guerrillas. I say that now we have 35,000, including more than 3,000 female recruits. Although the Turkish army has around one million men, it has been forced by the conflict to extend the length of its national service. Our guerrilla losses are a little more than 3,000. If you include Turkish losses, the total dead is more than 10,000.

In 1993 the PKK executed 33 unarmed Turkish soldiers, ending a ceasefire. Why?

The ceasefire wasn't really operative at the time: 120 guerrillas and civilians had been killed by the state during that period. Many Kurdish villages were burned down. A ceasefire doesn't seem feasible at the moment but we are always ready to talk.

Would the PKK like a Kurdish state to include Kurds in Syria, Iraq and Iran?

It's our ultimate goal, but our main struggle is in Turkish-occupied Kurdistan. Kurdistan is over 500,000 square kilometres. We believe that the borders will be determined by the struggle, by the people themselves. Talking about borders now might create more problems – it can be discussed in the future.

Couldn't it be argued that by cooperating with Turkey and the West, Kurds in Iraq have achieved more than you? After all, they have their own parliament.

Kurds in Iraq may have their own parliament but have you ever seen a parliament which can't fly its own flag? That part of Kurdistan has the potential to become the first truly independent part of Kurdistan. We are settling among Kurds in Iraq and trying to persuade them to join us.

The PKK is often described as a Marxist-Leninist organization. Is this accurate?

Our aim is to fight for freedom, to break the mould of one thousand years of slavery. Whatever you want to call us, this is what we are.

We know the PKK commander Abdullah Öcalan is hiding in Syria. Isn't the PKK just a tool being used by Syria and Iran to destabilize Turkey?

It's a free movement, not under the control of any other. If you can prove that any country provides us with military aid – well, prove it. The PKK is the bridge for the Kurdish people to cross from slavery into freedom.

What is the situation in southeast Turkey?

Everybody has been talking about Bosnia but nobody seems to realize what is happening in Kurdistan, which is five times the size of Bosnia. The extent of attacks on civilians is so great that over two thousand villages have been emptied and almost two thousand civilians have been killed. The state is carrying out a forced migration, trying to break the ties between the guerrillas and the people; but this creates potential for us in the cities.

When were you last in Kurdistan to know all this?

Even though we are here, every hour we are living in Kurdistan. I've been abroad just over one year but it doesn't make any difference. This is the PKK's nature, this is how we fight: one day we are in one place, the next day somewhere else.

When did you start fighting?

I've been fighting for the Kurdish nation for the last twenty years and now I'm over forty. I joined the PKK when I was a trade unionist. I was in prison for ten years, I completed my sentence and then I left Turkey. My movement sent me here. I could be in the mountains, in Kurdistan – wherever the movement wants me to work.

You say the Turkish Government can't win this war, but can the PKK really win it?

I don't think you can even question whether a nation which is fighting and standing up can be defeated. It is wrong in the eyes of history. The Kurdish nation deserves freedom like any other nation. We fight believing in this.

But thousands have been killed in ten years of war. Aren't Kurds tired of fighting?

The Turkish casualty figures are lies. Kurdish people feel the pain of their slavery so much, they are not tired of fighting. As we approach the end of the struggle, they will become more determined to support us and will not give in to tiredness.

In June 1994 a British tourist died after a PKK bomb exploded in a Turkish holiday resort. How can you justify the murder of civilians?

Of course we felt sad about that. We don't even like it when someone has a nosebleed. For the last two years we have been making calls, saying 'don't go to Turkey – it's a war zone'. Why are tourists still going there? They don't go to Bosnia, they shouldn't go to Turkey. After the war, when we have a free Kurdistan, then tourists can come. Tourists should know that every dollar they spend becomes a bullet against our people.

Did the PKK commander-in-chief Abdullah Öcalan order the brutal murder of six Turkish teachers in southeast Turkey in September 1994?

No. The leadership doesn't order individual actions. Everybody in the struggle reports to our leader to get his perspectives and tell him what's happening.

If the PKK commits atrocities then won't people in Europe and Turkey think it's a bloodthirsty terrorist organization?

The word 'terrorist' is wrong. We want our freedom, our country, our identity, but our demand for nationhood is branded as terrorism. We only want our name; Kurds don't yet have a name in the world and we want to shout it out. It hasn't been clarified whether those six teachers were killed by our guerrillas. If they were, well we've made announcements saying that we don't want Turkish education in Kurdistan. The Turkish state is the real killer for sending teachers.

Do all Kurds think like you?

Every nation has its betrayers, its dishonourable people. As soon as people betray their nation they are not part of it. They are not human.

Do you accept that the PKK commits atrocities?

Absolutely not. We have been forced to take up arms, not because we want to. There may have been one or two isolated incidents but this is not our practice. We are a humanitarian movement trying to secure the freedom of a nation.

If Kurds were allowed to learn their language in schools and could have Kurdish radio and television, and if the human rights situation improved, wouldn't that be enough to satisfy Kurds in Turkey?

The Turkish state says 'let's end the war and then we will open Kurdish schools'. Why didn't they give us those things before the war? This is just another pretext for invading our country and annihilating our people. Kurdish people are no longer naive and silent like they were twenty years ago. Now they have an organization, a leadership and a war and they won't be tricked.

Does the PKK want to destabilize Turkey, destroy it?

I have every right to destroy a country which destroys mine. But our aim is to let neither Kurdistan nor Turkey be destroyed; a peace between two proud, honourable nations.

Are you going to spread the war to Europe?

We have no intention of waging a war in Europe, but especially in Germany and France there are problems when police attack us. If European countries insist on supporting Turkey they will find the whole Kurdish people against them. We will fight to the last bullet, to the last person. The international community has to interfere and say stop. If the problem isn't solved, then there will be no stability in the Middle East.

What role do Kurds living in Europe play in your struggle?

There are more than one million Kurds in Europe: 80 per cent are with our party. They give financial support – the donations are voluntary, continuous and quite high. Thousands of Kurds in Europe want to go to the mountains, to take part in the war. Our main aim for the next year [1995] is to train and educate 10,000 Kurds in Europe.

Do you think there will be a Kurdish state in your lifetime?

It's not appropriate to put a timescale on it but I do believe my people will be free. There is a limit to how much any state can take. Even with the second largest army in NATO, the Turks can't succeed against us. Inflation in Turkey is high, and the Turks' prestige abroad is suffering. If the Turks look at their collapsing economy, then they may negotiate, they may see that they are wasting their resources.

What are your plans for 1995?

Guerrillas will continue attacking Turkish targets as long as the state doesn't approve a political solution. The war is being intensified – next year is a year of liberation and freedom.

The Wild East

I was not able to photograph freely in southeast Turkey because of the vigilant and hostile military presence (pages 98–9). It was a question of photographing, in a covert manner, what I could whenever the opportunity arose (100, 101). I decided early on that since access to events was limited, I would have to try to tell my story by relating the sense of misery and fear which is part of daily life for Kurdish civilians and which soon becomes familiar to any traveller in these troubled lands. There is no freedom of movement and a government press card means little or nothing to the security forces operating in what is effectively a police state. Soldiers, police and gendarmerie are everywhere and it is impossible to travel more than a few kilometres around the countryside without running into a roadblock at which one is met at best with suspicion but more likely with hostility. You come to accept as normal the ferret-like followers and the policemen loitering in the hotel foyer. Surveillance and harassment are the norm, as ordinary as the squalor of the shanty towns, queuing for welfare hand-outs at the Town Hall in Diyarbakır or studying in the improvised graveyard that looks down from the muddy hillside to the plains which reach out towards the Syrian border. There is resignation and hopelessness in the eyes of the people endorsed by the forlorn landscape which hosts the fugitives from the war (102–11, 122–3).

The consequences of the conflict in Kurdistan are now being felt in Europe. The issue was brought to the attention of the world in 1991 after the failed insurrection against Saddam Hussein by the Iraqi Kurds which drove hundreds of thousands of refugees into Turkey (116–21). At first, the Turks refused to allow the Kurds to cross the border but international pressure forced the Government to change its mind and resulted eventually in the creation of the safe haven in north Iraq. The growing number of Kurds living in Europe as either guest workers or asylum seekers (112–15) will ensure that their struggle remains in the news. Their presence has already led to extreme political protest and is likely to result in further acts of terrorism.

The family in the cover photograph had run away from their village following an attack by soldiers who took eleven men away with them (now presumed dead). We met the family by chance in Diyarbakır, after an abortive attempt to reach their village, and Jonathan read to them a roll call of those reported missing. The despair and disbelief registered on their faces will probably turn to hatred and, naturally, a desire for revenge.

Kurdish politicians have been threatened and frightened by the assassination of colleagues to such an extent that their parties did not contest local elections in 1994 (124–5). The revivalist Islamic movement has taken full advantage of the situation and has made dramatic electoral gains. The crisis in a country that purports to be a democracy, yet commits to trial its writers and MPs for supposedly having contact with or writing about the PKK (126–7), will not be eased until the Turks reappraise their belief in the philosophy of Mustafa Kemal Atatürk and try to incorporate a multi-ethnic humanistic ideal into their approach to the Kurdish question (128).

I would like to thank Steve Mayes for his encouragement and critical advice, my colleagues and friends at Network Photographers for their continued support and John Reardon of the *Observer* who asked me to go in the first place.

Roger Hutchings
June 1995

Soldiers patrol the streets of Cizre during Newroz 1995.

Above Police search a Kurd at a
police roadblock near Bismil: all
travellers are treated with extreme
suspicion.

Right Turkish police presence at a
political rally in Diyarbakır.

A mother and her sick child at a shanty town in Diyarbakır.

Children in a shanty town in Diyarbakır.

A child newly arrived in Diyarbakır from the countryside.

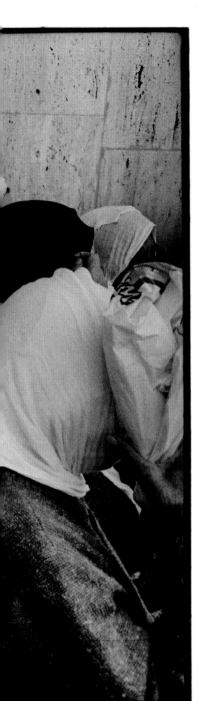

Women waiting for charity handouts in Diyarbakır.

There is little to do while waiting for charity handouts in Diyarbakır.

Outlands: this forlorn landscape has become home to Kurdish refugees.

Night falls on
the outskirts of
Diyarbakır.

Right
Conditions in
the shanty
towns are
squalid.

108

Kurdish girls
studying in a
makeshift
graveyard.

Right A barren
hillside where
Kurds are
trying to build a
settlement.

Right Kurds on their way to Adana.

110

Tower blocks
built to house
the influx of
people arriving
in Diyarbakır
to escape the
war.

Right A mother
and child watch
and wait in a
shanty town.

Political protest in London: a Kurd seeking asylum burned himself to death in custody while waiting for his case to be heard.

Kurds protest in London
after the Turkish
invasion of north Iraq
in 1995.

114

A torture victim has physiotherapy at the Medical Foundation for the Victims of Torture in London.

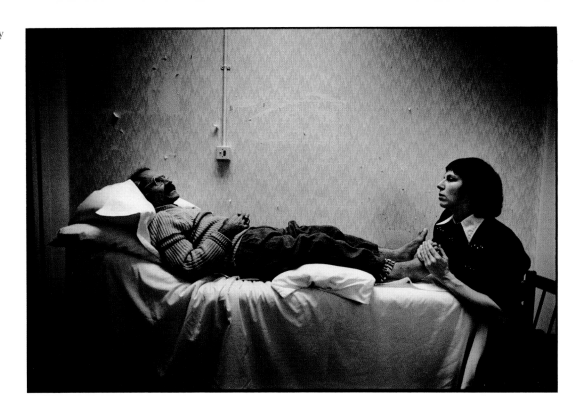

Hunger striker outside the Home Office in London after the arrest of PKK spokesman Kani Yılmaz.

115

After a failed insurrection against
Saddam Hussein in 1991, Iraqi
Kurds fled to Turkey. International
pressure led to the establishment
of a safe haven in north Iraq.

Iraqi Kurdish refugee in Turkey.

Turkish Red Crescent giving food to Kurds from Iraq.

At first, Turkish soldiers refused to let Iraqi Kurds cross the frontier.

An Iraqi Kurdish refugee tries to dry her blanket on a rock.

Right and below Çelebi village –
burned down by the Turkish army.

Left The shocked villagers of
Alacıköy listen as Jonathan
Rugman reads out the names of
relatives who have disappeared.

Left Kurdish parties were too intimidated to contest the election.

Right and far right Elections in the southeast saw great gains for the Islamic Welfare Party.

Above The defence lawyers in an Ankara court where eight Kurdish MPs were on trial for alleged contact with PKK members.

Kurdish MPs Orhan Doğan and
Ahmet Türk.

Kurdish MPs in the dock at
Ankara State Security Court.

127

Atatürk – father of modern Turkey.

Atatürk's statue, Atatürk Boulevard, Ankara.